To my colleagues and friends in the
RE Council of England and Wales.

Trevor Cooling, September 2010

Theos
The public theology think tank

what Theos is

Theos is a public theology think tank which exists to undertake research and provide commentary on social and political arrangements. We aim to impact opinion around issues of faith and belief in society. We were launched in November 2006 with the support of the Archbishop of Canterbury, Dr Rowan Williams, and the Cardinal Archbishop of Westminster, Cardinal Cormac Murphy-O'Connor. Our first report *"Doing God": A Future for Faith in the Public Square* examined the reasons why faith will play an increasingly significant role in public life.

what Theos stands for

Society is embarking on a process of de-secularisation. Interest in spirituality is increasing across Western culture. Faith is on the agenda of both government and the media. In the arts, humanities and social sciences there are important intellectual developments currently taking place around questions of values and identity. Theos speaks into this new context. Our perspective is that faith is not just important for human flourishing and the renewal of society, but that society can only truly flourish if faith is given the space to do so. We reject notions of a sacred-secular divide.

what Theos works on

Theos undertakes research across a wide range of subject areas. We analyse social and political change and offer interesting new angles and alternative perspectives on the issues that matter.

what Theos provides

Theos provides:

- a research and publishing programme,
- conferences, seminars and lectures,
- outreach to university, college and school students,
- news, information and analysis to media companies and other opinion formers, with a one-stop information line available to journalists,
- regular email bulletins,
- other related activities.

In addition to our independently driven work, Theos provides research, analysis and advice to individuals and organisations across the private, public and not-for-profit sectors. Our unique position within the think tank sector means that we have the capacity to develop proposals that carry values - with an eye to demonstrating what really works. Our staff and consultants have strong public affairs experience, an excellent research track record and a high level of theological literacy. We are practised in campaigning, media relations, detailed policy development and effecting policy change.

www.theosthinktank.co.uk

Doing God in Education

by Trevor Cooling

Trevor Cooling is Professor of Christian Education at Canterbury Christ Church University. Prior to that he has worked as Director of the Transforming Lives Project, a principal lecturer in theology at the University of Gloucestershire, secondary adviser for the Diocese of Gloucester, chief executive of The Stapleford Centre and as a secondary school Head of RE. He is Treasurer of the RE Council of England and Wales and a well-known speaker and author on topics relating to religion and education. He is married to Margaret and has two sons, a foster-daughter and five grand-children.

Published by Theos in 2010
© Theos

ISBN-13 978-0-9562182-3-0

For further information and subscription details please contact:

Theos
Licence Department
77 Great Peter Street
London
SW1P 2EZ

T 020 7828 7777
E hello@theosthinktank.co.uk
www.theosthinktank.co.uk

contents

foreword

"Is there a Christian way to boil water?" So asked one wit on learning that there was apparently a distinctively Christian way to teach modern foreign languages.

The astonished question and its expected answer demonstrate with admirable clarity the dubious presuppositions on which many debates about the role of education in contemporary Britain take place. Of course there is not a *Christian* way of boiling water any more than there is a Christian way of teaching foreign languages, or any other subject for that matter. Teaching is about imparting accurate information, neutrally and objectively. It concerns itself with literacy, numeracy, scientific and historical facts, and the like. As soon as you imagine that there are narrowly ideological – worse *religious* – ways of imparting that information, you weaken your commitment to objectivity and open the door to all sorts of educational viruses that congregate under the heading of 'indoctrination'.

It is this conviction – that there is a self-evident, incontestable, neutral and objective way of teaching – that underpins almost every other aspect of the vexed debate concerning education in Britain today. What admissions procedures and criteria are acceptable for publicly-funded schools? What control over the curriculum should schools retain? Can and should there be Christian universities? All these issues are deliberated on the basis of certain, usually unexamined, presuppositions of what education is actually for.

Trevor Cooling's essay does examine them. Having worked as a secondary school Head of RE, a principal lecturer in theology at the University of Gloucestershire, Chief Executive of The Stapleford Centre, a Christian educational charity, and currently occupying the chair of Christian Education at Canterbury Christ Church University, he is well placed to analyse these issues.

The key point he makes is that education is not a neutral or objective process. What teachers teach and the way they teach it is heavily coloured by who they are and what they understand as being of value. This is not the same as saying that teaching is simply a leaf to be blown on every educational whim. Lessons must have content, curricula objectives, exams standards. That is just as it should be. Claiming that there is a distinctively Christian (or any other) way of teaching is not to say biology lessons should be opened up to fundamentalists advocating creationism just because they think it is 'valuable'.

Rather, to acknowledge the personal and therefore subjective nature of teaching is to recognise that a teacher's or a school's vision of the good will naturally inform the way they deal with children. Cooling gives a detailed example from the field of modern languages, as an apt response to the incredulous question above. The vocabulary taught, comprehensions given and role plays enacted often treat students as if they were interested in nothing more than tourism and consumption. When it comes to offering forgiveness or showing hospitality, human activities at least as common and significant as visiting and shopping, the language and practice often simply aren't there.

Examples extend beyond modern foreign languages. The content and method of teaching citizenship, or history, or biology, or mathematics are shaped by our ideas of what is good: of which virtues we should practice, what qualities we should value, ultimately of what kind of people we should be. Cooling repeatedly exposes the suppositions beneath our educational debates, in doing so making the case for a distinctive form of Christian education.

That form may be distinctive but not exclusive. At no point does Cooling imagine that the look of Christian education must be unique to Christian schools or universities. Thus the Church of England's vision of the virtues that should characterise Christian education – thankfulness, endurance, compassion, wisdom, humility and *koinonia* (best, though not perfectly, translated as fellowship) are distinctively Christian but they are not necessarily uniquely Christian. Many, as Cooling notes, would be welcomed by non-church schools.

Whether or not such virtues are shared, the point is not only that they are authentic outworkings of the Christian worldview but that they are positive outworkings too. The task before us is not simply to acknowledge that there are distinctive ways of teaching and that those ways must, grudgingly, be given oxygen in a free society. It is that those ways make an appreciable and constructive contribution to our common life.

It is only when we have recognised this that we can engage with neuralgic issues like funding or admissions policy in a genuinely open and fair manner. Church schools – and by association those of other faiths, although Cooling focuses on the former in this report – are not the egregious examples of special pleading that secularist rhetoric claims. Rather they are a legitimate and positive expression of the moral and metaphysical commitments of a large number – arguably the majority – of the British population. Moreover, those commitments are not simply examples of stubborn self-interest but in fact comprise a valuable contribution to the common good from which we all benefit.

Thus, in answer to our incredulous wit above: there is a Christian way of boiling water. It is to boil only that which you need because, underpinning such a simple and mundane act, there is moral commitment to the responsible use of resources (water, electricity) that is demanded by a metaphysical commitment to steward God's creation wisely. Such an attitude to boiling water is not *exclusively* Christian, of course. There will be many who do not share the Christian faith who would be minded to do precisely the same thing. But that is good. Christians should welcome those who seek to respect God's creation, no matter what their motivations. The key point is that whether you are boiling water or teaching foreign languages, there are *particular* ways of doing so, ways that are based on *particular* moral convictions that contribute positively to the common good.

Most of us will fail to spot the convictions that underlie most of the simple, mundane acts that make up our daily lives. Even the most pious of Christians rarely thinks of God when making a cup of tea. It is only careful attention to the way we understand the world that will alert us to such convictions and commitments. A proper Christian education makes a vital contribution to generating that attention.

Trevor Cooling's report is an important, reasonable, balanced and thoughtful contribution to the case for Christian education. It deserves to be read by those who seek to shape Christian education in our public life and those who want to eradicate it.

Nick Spencer
Director or Studies, Theos

introduction

Is prayer a form of bullying? Apparently yes, if you are a teacher and if Olive Jones' experience is anything to go by.

Olive is a maths teacher working with children too ill to attend mainstream school.[1] She is a Christian for whom prayer is part of the warp and woof of life. In 2009, on a visit to the home of one of her pupils who was undergoing treatment for cancer she offered to say a prayer. That offer elicited a complaint from the parents and Olive was suspended. Sharing your own beliefs whilst employed as a teacher was allegedly seen as form of bullying. As a maths teacher there was no place for her praying in the workplace.

As with any incident like this, there are two sides to the story. From the side of the parents and employer, this was a case of an insensitive person who was not suitably professional in relation to her own personal religious beliefs. Her behaviour caused distress to a vulnerable and seriously ill teenager. From Olive Jones' perspective, she saw a young person suffering and desperately wanted to help. Her own experience was of a God who answered prayer. She knew that the girl's family were not religious people, but she felt she could bring some hope. She made a tentative offer to pray knowing that many people who are not Christians appreciate this as a gesture of solidarity. However, when that was declined she took things no further out of respect for the family.

The end of the story is that Olive was offered her job back. Cases like hers are increasingly common and often attract intense media attention. The appropriate handling of religious beliefs in education is now a very controversial matter. As the next case study shows, this is even the case at the highest levels of academia.

In October 2008 another media storm had exploded, this time around Michael Reiss, the Education Officer for the Royal Society, Professor of Science Education at the Institute of Education at London University and an Anglican clergyman. In a public lecture, Reiss suggested that if a student asked a question about creationism in a science lesson, the teacher should not dismiss it outright as wrong-headed, but should engage with the question as a legitimate exploration of a worldview.[2] Eminent Royal Society members, among them Nobel Prize winners, were outraged and protested vociferously. What seemed particularly objectionable to some was that Reiss had ever been appointed to the Royal Society position, given that he was ordained.[3] As a result of the publicity storm,

Reiss agreed to step down as Education Officer because his views were "open to misinterpretation" and therefore potentially damaging to the credibility of the Royal Society as the UK's national academy of science.[4]

The problem was that science, as far as the Royal Society was concerned, has no truck with creationism. It has no "scientific basis and should not be part of the science curriculum". By suggesting that teachers should engage with creationism in the science classroom, Reiss was open to the charge of giving non-science the status of science. That was a cardinal sin and Reiss fell on his sword for it.

These are just two examples of a challenge faced by everyone in education today. How is religious belief to be handled when there is such diversity of views in society? Since education is largely funded by the state, should religious beliefs have any place in the educational institutions of a religiously diverse democracy? Should teachers and lecturers be free to express their views on matters of faith or should professional integrity mean that they keep quiet?

the purpose of education

The questions that lie at the heart of this debate are "what is the purpose of education?" and "how does religious belief relate to that?" The answer developed in this report can be illustrated through considering two well-known scientists.

Richard Dawkins and Francis Collins are both leading biologists with prestigious reputations. They are also both vocal in expressing their views on matters of religious belief. Dawkins is an atheist who believes passionately that evolution gives a total explanation for the nature of life on earth. For Dawkins, God is a delusion.[5] Francis Collins, who was the Director of the Human Genome Project, in contrast is a Christian convert. For him the natural world does not make sense unless one sees it as the result of God's design.[6] For Dawkins design in the natural world is an illusion. For Collins it is inherent.

Dawkins and Collins are scientific colleagues. They share the same knowledge base and can work with integrity within the same discipline. Their different religious beliefs make no difference to their professional capacity to work as biologists. There is a shared scientific activity which is based on rational principles. However, they differ fundamentally when it comes to the *meaning and significance* they attribute to their shared enterprise. For Collins it only makes sense in a world where there is a Creator, but for Dawkins it leads him to believe that God does not exist. Dawkins and Collins have both written books intended to persuade others of the truth of their beliefs. For both of them the shared activity of science is important, but the interpretation of the meaning and significance of science is even more so; indeed, the two activities are inextricably related. What then are the implications of this observation for education?

Faith schools are a significant factor in the current educational scene. Their existence raises the question of how their ethos relates to their educational role. For example, Church of England schools are encouraged to explore how the curriculum might be "distinctively Christian". Science teachers sometimes object to this on the grounds that the purpose of science lessons is to teach young people the discipline of science, not to engage with debates about religious belief. Those, they argue, should happen elsewhere in the curriculum, if indeed they have any place in education.

But what is being said here? The argument seems to be that science lessons are *purely* about passing on the facts of science and inducting students into scientific method. That means that the debate between Collins and Dawkins about meaning and significance is being treated as of no consequence for science teachers. And yet Dawkins and Collins as professional scientists are committed enough to that debate to give it considerable time and energy. They know it matters. Why should not science lessons contribute to the wider educational task of helping pupils develop their understanding of meaning and significance in life? Why should such debates be confined (or perhaps relegated) to Religious Education (RE) lessons and assemblies?

> *This report argues that learning to make judgments about the meaning and significance of what we learn is, actually, what education is all about.*

Interestingly, discussions about the nature of RE in schools throw significant light on this question.[7] Good RE teachers don't just teach the facts about religion, but put great emphasis on helping students to make their own judgments about the meaning and significance of religious belief. This is the *learning from* dimension of the subject. That's why it is called religious *education* and not just religion. Why then is the curriculum subject science not called science *education*? Maybe a change of name is needed because the value of teaching science in schools should lie not just in learning scientific information, but in developing the ability to make judgments about the meaning and significance of science. In other words, science in schools should be contributing to *pupils' development as persons* and not just to their knowledge of science. The debate between Dawkins and Collins is too important to be ignored by science teachers. *This report argues that learning to make judgments about the meaning and significance of what we learn is, actually, what education is all about.* This is expressed evocatively in the following letter from a holocaust survivor written to the United Nations about the importance of studying history:

Dear Teacher

I am a survivor of a concentration camp. My eyes saw what no man should witness:

Gas chambers built by learned engineers; children poisoned by educated physicians; infants killed by trained nurses; women and babies shot by high school graduates; so I am suspicious of education.

> *Reading, writing and arithmetic are important only if they serve to make our children more human.*

My request is: help your students to become human. Your efforts must never produce learned monsters, skilled psychopaths, educated Eichmanns.

Reading, writing and arithmetic are important only if they serve to make our children more human. [8]

the purpose of this report

This report examines the vexed question of how religious beliefs should be dealt with in education in Britain today. This debate manifests itself in all sorts of ways. The headlines are grabbed when, for example, a pressure group tries to abolish Christian worship in schools, or when a high profile figure makes a television documentary objecting to government funding for faith schools, or when a science teacher reveals that he or she is a creationist, or when a primary school celebrates Halloween or when an RE syllabus requires schools to teach about paganism or humanism. Although attracting less media attention, it is also becoming a significant matter of debate in Higher Education with the Cathedral Group of universities (those with a Church foundation) becoming more vocal about their Christian distinctiveness.[9] However, underlying all these debates is one fundamental question: "How should debates about meaning and significance in life in wider society, particularly as interpreted by religious and non-religious belief systems, be handled in education?"

This report is based on the premise that grappling successfully with questions of meaning and significance contributes to developing into a healthy, balanced person and is a fundamentally important component of education.[10] This is not some specialist interest subject for the theological geeks but one that significantly affects the future well-being of society. How young people think about meaning and significance radically influences their values and behaviour. It affects the sort of citizen that they are and will become. It should, therefore, be of interest to everyone concerned with education policy.

Chapter 1 unpacks an influential undercurrent in the current debates, namely the twin emphases on "objectivity" and "fairness" that have shaped people's understanding of the purpose of education. It is argued that fairness in educational provision has become equated with being objective and therefore neutral. This, in turn, has been interpreted in terms of a humanist understanding of religious belief which treats it as irrelevant, indeed toxic, clutter. The result is that objective education is thereby unfair to those of religious faith because their faith is treated as private. Preference is too often given to a secular understanding of what it means to be human.

Chapter 2 offers a different understanding of the contribution of religious faith to human knowledge and learning. Through consideration of the influential concept of shared values it is argued that all knowing is underpinned by a worldview that can be religious or non-religious. Being nurtured in the faith of our family and community is inherent in the learning process. The claim that education can therefore be worldview neutral and that beliefs should be privatized is rejected.

Chapter 3 illustrates how an apparently technical subject like modern foreign languages is actually shaped by worldview beliefs and shows how Christian beliefs make a significant difference to teaching and learning. The insights gained are then applied to the debates that have surrounded the teaching of creationism and the conduct of school worship.

Chapter 4 returns to the theme of fairness and examines how state education can be fair even though it cannot be neutral. A pragmatic approach is proposed which recognizes that people can cooperate in achieving educational goals even though they might hold conflicting beliefs. It argues that the way forward is for people's religious and non-religious beliefs to be treated as a resource in the cause of promoting the common good through inclusive education and not as problematic clutter. Finally the criticism that faith-based education is discriminatory is itself critiqued. Lastly, chapter 5 outlines a number of possible practical implications resulting from the argument of the report.

Alistair Campbell once, as Tony Blair's communications guru, famously said, "we don't do God". This report presents the positive case for why "doing God" in education is the right thing.

introduction references

1. See http://www.dailymail.co.uk/news/article-1237601/Cancer-patient-left-traumatised-Christian-teacher-Olive-Joness-offer-pray-her.html for one version of this widely reported story.

2. I am using the word creationism to describe the Christian position which asserts that God created the world literally as described in Genesis.

3. See http://richarddawkins.net/articles/3119 for correspondence and comment.

4. See http://royalsociety.org/News.aspx?id=1153&terms=Michael+Reiss for the official statement

5. Dawkins' book *The God Delusion,* (Transworld Publishers, 2006) is probably his most influential statement of his beliefs.

6. This is not a creationist position, but embraces the belief that God is behind the evolutionary process. See Francis Collins, *The Language of God: A scientist provides evidence for belief* (Pocket Books, 2007).

7. See, for example, *RE: the non-statutory national framework,* (QCA, 2004) and *Religious Education guidance in English Schools: Non-statutory guidance 2010* (http://www.teachernet.gov.uk/teachingandlearning/subjects/re/guidance/).

8. Widely available on a number of websites.

9. This is a new name for the universities that belong to the Council of Church Universities and Colleges. For a recent discussion of issues see Michael Wright and James Arthur (eds.), *Leadership in Christian Higher Education,* (Imprint Academic, 2010).

10. See, for example, Richard Layard, *Happiness: Lessons from a New Science* (Penguin Books, 2005) pp. 22-23, 73 and *The Formation of Virtues and Dispositions in 16-19 year olds,* a research project of the *Learning for Life Programme* (http://www.learningforlife.org.uk/research-projects/learning-for-life-research-reports/view/?id=1).

fairness or objectivity

the emphasis on objectivity

In 1972 Paul Hirst, then Professor of Education at the University of Cambridge, published what was to be a highly influential article.[1] His assertion was that "there has emerged in our society a concept of education which makes the whole idea of Christian education a kind of nonsense". This idea shapes the debate about religion and education to this day.

The significance of Hirst's paper lies in the justification that he offered for his assertion. This rested on the belief that a crucial feature in modern thinking about education is the secularization of knowledge and the consequent rejection of reliance on religious beliefs. A key element in Hirst's notion of secular knowledge was the concept of objectivity, which defined what it meant to be rational. Rationality, as Hirst presented it, is a *universal and shared* human characteristic, which transcends cultural differences. It is a key element in what it means to be human. To be rational is, he asserted, to participate in acquiring the objective knowledge, ideas and ways of thinking that are common to all right and free-thinking people. If an idea is derived from rationality alone, it is a universal idea, a shared human idea, an objective idea, a neutral idea, and a secular idea. Such an idea is not then contentious, unlike those that rest on religious beliefs.

On this basis Hirst later distinguished between primitive approaches to education, which consist of passing on the contentious beliefs and ideas of particular cultures, and sophisticated approaches, which are concerned only with transmitting the universal norms of rationality and objective knowledge.[2] The difference between them was that sophisticated education promotes autonomy, by which he meant making decisions according to rational principles alone, whereas a primitive approach does not. Christian education, or indeed any faith-based education, is a form of primitive education because it seeks to transmit contentious beliefs. For Hirst "true", i.e. sophisticated, education is independent of any of the particularities of religious belief.

Hirst's views lead to one important conclusion. It is fine, in sophisticated education, to teach *about* religion because pupils need to know and understand people's religious beliefs and practices. RE is therefore a worthy subject, helping pupils to understand beliefs and to make their own autonomous choices. *However, what is not legitimate is to make religious belief the basis of an educational ethos or to permit religion to have a shaping influence on the curriculum*. This would be to allow religion to reach beyond its rightful remit. Religious belief is a private matter that should not impinge on the objective, educational task of promoting rationality. The now-adopted policy of the Church of England that its schools and universities should be *distinctively Christian* would have horrified Hirst.[3]

How relevant are Hirst's views forty years on? Recent research on the attitudes of Christian and atheist students training to teach RE in secondary schools suggests that their influence is still considerable.[4] The Christian students were generally hesitant about sharing their faith in their lessons, believing it was unprofessional to do so. The atheist students, in stark contrast, were happy to share their beliefs thinking that made a positive contribution to the lesson. They apparently felt that because their beliefs were secular, not religious, that made them objective and therefore neutral.

This report argues that, even though you would be unlikely to find people directly quoting Hirst today, his conclusions are very influential in current thinking about faith and education. The perception of these student RE teachers reflects a consensus in the wider world of education.

It argues that the problem with the Hirstian position is that it preferences a secular view of meaning and significance over a religious one. In the debate between Richard Dawkins and Francis Collins, it means that Dawkins' atheist view of science is being promoted and Collins' view is being excluded. The question is, is this fair and appropriate in an education system that is serving the needs of a religiously-diverse society?

humanism and the argument from fairness

Humanism is an influential, non-religious belief system. In education it has a significant voice through the work of the British Humanist Association (BHA), which has advanced two types of argument in its campaigning on education.[5]

It opposes discrimination on the basis of religion on the grounds that it violates the human rights of non-religious people. In the cause of equality and diversity it has argued that *fairness* in a religiously plural democracy demands that no belief system should be privileged in education so that pupils from the different communities that make up Britain will all be affirmed and flourish. Fairness also requires that pupils should be free to create their own identity and not have their beliefs "directed" by an institution of the state. Religious views should not therefore be privileged over non-religious views, nor should pupils or staff be discriminated against in admissions or appointments policies on the basis of religion. On these grounds, the BHA campaigns in particular for the inclusion of the study of humanism in RE and against faith schools. It would be against the privileging of Francis Collins' views over those of Richard Dawkins.

Using the fairness argument, the BHA has supported the humanist cause in education with two distinct justifications. On the one hand, humanists have placed themselves alongside minority religious communities, arguing for the right to be represented in the curriculum as another significant minority belief position. On the other hand, they have argued that humanists reflect the views of the silent majority. Despite the fact that there are relatively few signed-up, active humanists

It is a good thing to encourage members of the different belief communities to play as full a part as possible in promoting the public good.

it claims, on the basis of a poll, that 17 million people in Britain hold humanist beliefs. The BHA claims to be representing this silent majority and seeking to protect their rights in education in the face of what it regards as the illegitimate privileging of minority religious beliefs.[6] Either way, whether it is on behalf of the humanist minority or of the silent majority, the BHA has enjoyed considerable success in advancing this fairness argument. For example, although there are still legal restrictions on humanist representatives serving on the local groups that oversee RE in England and Wales, it is now widely recognized that secular beliefs should feature in RE syllabuses.[7]

The BHA is a founding partner in Accord, a coalition of religious and non-religious partners including the Christian think tank Ekklesia, the Association of Teachers and Lecturers, the Hindu Academy and British Muslims for Secular Democracy.[8] It describes itself as follows:

> The Accord Coalition was launched in early September 2008 to bring together religious and non-religious organisations campaigning for an end to religious discrimination in school staffing and admissions. The coalition also campaigns for a fair and balanced RE curriculum and the removal of the requirement for compulsory collective worship but does not take a position for or against faith schools in principle.[9]

The fairness argument is the main plank of Accord's campaigning. It argues that, in a plural society, education should promote equality of opportunity and human rights, and oppose discrimination. Whether or not a pupil has a place in a particular school, or a member of staff is recruited for or promoted within a school should not depend on matters of religious belief. Furthermore they support pupil autonomy, being committed to education which enables children to "develop their own identities and sense of place in the world."[10] They believe that, through practicing unfair religious discrimination in school admissions and staff recruitment, most faith schools contribute to the development of a society where people from religious communities live parallel lives.[11] If we are to have a socially cohesive society, they argue, we need inclusive educational institutions where people of all faiths and none learn side by side. The fairness argument is therefore widely influential and is not specific to humanism.

This report accepts that the fairness argument is basically sound given the context of Britain as a diverse democracy comprised of people of many religious faiths and none. It rests on the assumption that it is a good thing to encourage members of the different belief communities to play as full a part as possible in promoting the public good. Applying that idea to humanists, it follows that they have as much right to appropriate representation of their beliefs in the curriculum and to influence educational policy as anyone else. Fairness should be pursued.[12]

humanism and the argument from objectivity

The second type of argument advanced by the BHA is of a totally different order, however. In its campaigning the BHA has sought to limit the wider influence of religious belief on the ethos and culture of schools on the philosophical grounds that education ought to be *objective* rather than inculcating partisan views. This stance is reflected in BHA campaigns on issues such as school worship, faith schools and the teaching of creationism in science lessons, rather than in it is campaigning on RE, where there is greater dependence on the fairness argument.

In order to unpack this objectivity argument, two texts from the pen of the humanist philosopher Professor Richard Norman will be reviewed.[13] Both of these are distributed by the BHA. They offer a significant insight into the humanist belief system.

In his book *On Humanism*, Norman explains humanist belief concerning what it means to be human. Humans are, he claims, characterized by their capacity for rational thought. They flourish when that rationality is promoted. In the case of morality, a basic component of human rationality, this rational nature is evidenced by the shared moral values which are clearly identifiable in the midst of cultural and religious diversity. According to Norman, these shared values "are entirely independent of religious belief".[14] They are, in contrast to faith-based values, objective and are therefore universal. In a startling metaphor, Norman states that religious beliefs are "clutter" and "humanists will want to remove the clutter".[15] Furthermore Norman asserts that, "there has long been a free-thinking tradition in this country which has questioned religious belief".[16] Not only, therefore, are religious beliefs "clutter" but to question them apparently characterizes "free-thinking". Such views are clearly Hirstian.

There are, then, two arguments used by humanists in thinking about education; firstly, the fairness argument, which seeks parity of treatment and, secondly, the objectivity argument, which rests on the distinctively humanist assertion that religious beliefs are irrelevant "clutter". The critical question for this report is the relationship between these two arguments from fairness and objectivity.

At first sight, the argument from fairness appears to be the primary consideration. For example, in *The Case for Secularism*, the work Norman edited for the Humanist Philosophers' Group, the idea that society could be based on Christian values is said to be acceptable in principle "as long as the religion really is shared".[17] However, as soon as the religion becomes contested, then it is unacceptable to impose religious values. They are no longer "shared". This, it is believed, is the situation in modern democracies and is the reason why it is no longer appropriate to have Christian schools. This line of reasoning clearly depends on the fairness argument and appears to trump the objectivity argument.

But, in reality, for humanists the Hirstian argument from objectivity trumps the fairness argument. From this point of view, an education based on Christian values *would always be regarded as inappropriate,* even if most people shared those Christian values and whatever fairness appeared to demand, because Christian beliefs are "clutter". For humanists, Dawkins' position always trumps that of Collins on the grounds of the objective argument. Considering the idea of autonomy will illustrate the point.

autonomy

Humanists are committed to promoting autonomy.[18] For example, in the BHA billboard campaign in November 2009, posters of happy children were accompanied by the slogan, "Please don't label me. Let me grow up and choose for myself."[19] Children, humanists believe, ought to make up their own minds and not be "indoctrinated" into religious belief. But is this commitment to autonomy based on a belief in the importance of *fairness* or the importance of *objectivity*? Do humanists simply want young people to be free to choose for themselves or do they actually want them to be unencumbered by religious "clutter" so as to be objective, rational free-thinkers?

In *The Case for Secularism* the authors define autonomy as "individuals making their own choices about the most important things in their own lives."[20] This seems to be a clear expression of the aspiration for fairness. However, in the same publication the equating of "free-thinking" with "questioning religious belief" suggests that real autonomy for humanists lies in freeing oneself from unnecessary religious "clutter".[21] For humanists the "objectivity" argument trumps the "fairness" argument. Hence their outright opposition to faith schools.

It is important to appreciate that this is not considered unfair by humanists because, following the Hirstian logic, objective education is neutral, based on shared rationality. It focuses on what is common to all humans and simply leaves out the religious "clutter". This "clutter", properly respecting fairness, is studied in RE and religious people are free to pursue it in their own communities. But education itself should not be shaped by such "clutter"; rather it should be objective and therefore neutral. This idea is enunciated in the education policy document of the BHA when it states that "in our ideal society religious belief would be a purely private matter" and "schools would be strictly neutral on religious matters."[22] Having experienced neutral, objective education, pupils would then be in a better position to choose for themselves. Neutral, objective education is therefore totally fair since it favours no particular belief system, be that religious or non-religious.

The humanist resistance to "doing God" in education therefore rests on the argument that religious belief is private "clutter" that hampers the development of autonomy. Universal shared human values derived from the exercise of rationality alone should form the shaping influence in *fair* education. "Doing God" in education is inappropriate because it is both irrational and unfair. Only secular, objective education is both rational and fair.

However, in his book explaining humanism, the objectivist view of the nature of human knowledge from which this view of education is derived is depicted by Professor Norman as a *humanist belief about the nature of human knowledge*. It is a humanist depiction of what it means to be a human being. Neutral secularism based on the objectivity argument is a *distinctively humanist belief*. Despite his efforts to persuade them otherwise, Professor Norman himself recognizes that those of a religious disposition may not be convinced by his humanist arguments when he says "there is no single knock-down argument for secularism grounded in reasons which all religious believers can accept."[23] It is therefore not true when Professor Norman subsequently claims that the humanist arguments for secularism and a neutral state "do not appeal to any specifically humanist premises or assumptions".[24] We have already seen that using the fairness argument, humanists contend that they are a significant minority belief community. The adoption of a humanist view of human knowledge as a basis for public education is therefore as unfair as making Christian faith its basis.[25] To quote Richard Norman, "it is unfair that any one set of beliefs should have a privileged position."[26]

further concerns about religious faith

For humanists the fact that religious faith is irrational "clutter" alone makes it an unhealthy influence. And it certainly makes it an appropriate target for mockery. For example, Ariane Sherine, the instigator of the atheist bus advertising campaign, which encouraged people to enjoy a world where God probably doesn't exist, wrote an illuminating piece about how atheist teachers should approach Christmas. Her closing remark was:

> …you can totally mention the beardy bloke in the sky. Santa might not promise heaven and everlasting life, but he never floats the idea of hell as well [sic] (unless it's the hell of not getting what you wanted). He's all about giving and not receiving, is always jolly and cheery, and puts in lots of work for the simple reward of making people happy.[27]

Christian belief in God has elsewhere been equated with belief in celestial tea pots and tooth fairies.[28] Religious faith is clearly seen as superstitious nonsense by many humanists. Indeed even Richard Norman, whose careful writing is marked by a desire to comprehend the religious point of view, lapses into parody based on primitive representations of religious belief as, for example, when he accuses Christians of "dogmatic certainty", lacking modesty or when he describes god as "a divine being who commands us to live in the right way and will punish those who disobey."[29] If that is really how atheists think religious people view God, then it is not surprising that they are against "doing God" in education.

But the humanist concern is not just that religious faith is irrelevant, ridiculous "clutter", but that it is *toxic* clutter. Thus Richard Dawkins, in the preface to his best-selling *The God Delusion,* commented that he liked the newspaper advertising for a TV programme he made for Channel 4 because:

> It was a picture of the Manhattan skyline with the caption 'Imagine a world without religion.' What was the connection? The twin towers of the World Trade Center were conspicuously present.[30]

A world without religion would not have experienced the 9/11 atrocity.

This concern about the toxicity of religion is influential amongst policy makers. For example, Barry Sheerman, when chair of the parliamentary Select Committee of the then Department for Children, Schools and Families (DCSF), is on record as saying, when commenting on church schools, that "we all become a little more worried the more people take their faith seriously."[31] The implication seems to be that somehow *too much* religious commitment threatens community cohesion. So he prefers that it be relegated to a private zone where it won't threaten to supersede one's duty as a citizen.

Similar concerns about the toxic nature of "too much" religious commitment are expressed by the Accord coalition. For example, in the debate about the teaching of sex and relationships in schools that took place just before the General Election in 2010, the issue was whether faith schools should be allowed to teach from the point of view of their religious ethos. Accord campaigned against this being allowed. Their spokesperson, Rabbi Dr Jonathan Romain said:

> It is astonishing that the Government plans to allow state-funded schools to teach the subject from one religious viewpoint. Ed Balls is implicitly condoning homophobia in schools.[32]

The assumption seems to be that the type of religious faith that aspires to establish schools with a religious character will, inevitably, be homophobic. A similar view is expressed by Rev Richard Kirker, when he writes, "faith schools have become a tarnished brand as within the majority of them stalks the unacceptable side of faith – unchecked homophobia. No public money should be used to condone covert discrimination on the grounds of sexual orientation."[33]

That the perceived toxic nature of religion might be fuelling opposition to religious faith having a shaping role in education is supported by the number of times Northern Ireland is mentioned in debates over faith schools. It seems self-evident to many that faith schools breed intolerance. Interestingly it is usually not mentioned that many of the integrated schools in Northern Ireland are themselves faith schools having a distinctive Christian ethos, although they are not divided along *denominational* lines.[34] The idea of "doing God" in public education creates discomfort in such a climate.

conclusion

Arguments from both fairness and objectivity have been cited by those who campaign against faith schools and other manifestations of religion influencing the nature and ethos of education. However, it appears that consistently objectivity trumps fairness. In the argument from objectivity, religion is portrayed as irrelevant, possibly toxic, "clutter". Fairness goes as far as allowing this "clutter" to be studied in RE, but education itself should be shaped only by neutral, objective, secular thinking.

This position would hold water if this was a genuinely neutral, and therefore fair, position. But it is not. It is in reality an education the nature and ethos of which is shaped by distinctively humanist beliefs concerning what it means to be human. The CEO of the BHA is clearly aware of this.

> The BHA campaigns for totally inclusive schools for children of all faiths and none. In our view, many inclusive community schools are already more or less humanist in their ethos and values. If compulsory collective worship was ended and RE became universally objective, fair and balanced, community schools would indeed be humanist in all but name, open and accommodating to all.[35]

That's unfair. For those of religious faith, the openness and accommodation comes at the price of having one's faith treated as irrational and toxic "clutter".

The key issue in this debate is the relationship between religious belief and human rationality. Are objective, shared values really completely independent of religious belief as Professors Hirst and Norman argue? Or is education always shaped by particular beliefs? And if so can it ever be 'fair'? The rest of this report will be devoted to answering these questions. It will assume that fairness is the appropriate goal, but will reject the concept of neutrality and argue for the legitimacy of "doing God" in a way that is fair.

chapter 1 references

1. Paul Hirst, "Christian Education: a contradiction in terms?" in *Learning for Living,* 11.4 (1972) pp. 6-11. The arguments were developed in his *Moral Education in a Secular Society* (University of London Press, 1974).

2. Paul Hirst, "Education, Catechesis and the Church School" in *British Journal of Religious Education* 3.3 (1981) pp. 85-93.

3. See Archbishop's Council, *The Way Ahead; Church of England Schools in the new millennium* (Church House Publishing, 2001) and Church of England Board of Education, *Mutual expectations: The Church of England and Church Colleges/Universities* (Church of England, 2007).

4. Lynn Revell & Rosemary Walters, Christian student RE teachers, objectivity and professionalism, (Canterbury Christ Church University, 2010).

5. The other active campaigning organization is the National Secular Society. It is not discussed here because its position is straightforwardly anti-religious, whereas the BHA favours a partnership model.

6. See "Seventeen Million British Humanists" (British Humanist Association, 24 November 2006) http://www.humanism.org.uk/news/view/155. Retrieved 19 May 2008.

7. See Jacqueline Watson "Including secular philosophies such as humanism in locally agreed syllabuses for religious education" in *British Journal of Religious Education,* 32.1 (2010) pp. 5-18. The BHA has provided commendable resources to support this teaching. See http://www.humanismforschools.org.uk/.

8. http://www.accordcoalition.org.uk/.

9. See http://www.ekklesia.co.uk/node/11113.

10. http://accordcoalition.org.uk/aims/

11. Ibid.

12. See the Theos reports by Nick Spencer, *Neither Private nor Privileged* (2008) and Sean Oliver-Dee, *Religion and Identity: Divided loyalties?* (2009). See also my *Christian Vision for State Education* (SPCK, 1992) where I discuss the matter at length.

13. Richard Norman, *On Humanism* (Routledge, 2004) and *The Case for Secularism: a neutral state in an open society* (BHA, 2007), which Norman edited on behalf of the Humanist Philosophers' Group

14. Norman, *On Humanism,* p. 114.

15. Ibid, p. 118.

16. Ibid, p. 6.

17. Norman, ed., *The Case for Secularism,* op. cit. p. 5.

18. See, for example, Humanist Philosophers' Group, *Religious Schools: the case against* (BHA, 2001).

19. See http://www.humanism.org.uk/billboards.

20. Norman, ed., *The Case for Secularism,* p.10.

21. Ibid, p.6

22. From British Humanist Association, *A Better Way Forward* (Revised Edition, January 2006), p. 20. Available from http://www.humanism.org.uk/_uploads/documents/Betterwayforward2006.pdf.

23. Norman, *On Humanism,* p. 9.

24. Ibid, p. 16.

25. This is a clear example of what Jonathan Chaplin describes as the slide from procedural secularism to programmatic secularism. See *Talking God: The Legitimacy of Religious Public Reasoning* (Theos, 2008), chapter 1.

26. Norman, *On Humanism,* p. 13.

27. Ariane Sherine, "Deck the halls with the tales of unholy", *Times Educational Supplement,* 18/25 December 2009, p. 25.

28. See Dawkins, *The God Delusion,* op. cit. chapter 2.

29. Norman, *On Humanism,* pp. 135, 115.

30. Dawkins, *The God Delusion,* p. 23

31. *The Jonathan Dimbleby Big Debate – Religion in Schools,* broadcast 11 December 2007 on Teachers' TV. http://www.teachers.tv/videos/religion-in-schools.

32. Nicola Woolcock "Fury over U-turn on sex education in faith schools after amendment", *Times Online,* 19 February 2010. See http://www.timesonline.co.uk/tol/life_and_style/education/article7032728.ece .

33. http://www.accordcoalition.org.uk/index.php/our-supporters/.

34. Integrated schools are designed to be non-denominational in that they are not exclusively serving either the Protestant or Roman Catholic communities. But this does not mean they are not faith schools with a strong Christian ethos. They are a response to a political challenge not a religious challenge.

35. See http://www.humanism.org.uk/news/view/611.

why religious beliefs are not clutter

This chapter will argue that to treat religious beliefs as "clutter" is to misunderstand their significance in human knowledge. The importance of belief is well illustrated by a consideration of the much-loved concept of "shared values".

shared values

Shared values matter a lot in education because it is believed that, being independent of particular religious beliefs, they are non-controversial and are considered to be the epitome of objectivity in education. They are therefore perceived to be both *objective and fair* because they reflect a genuine consensus that can form an uncontentious basis for public education. But is this so?

Those responsible for education policy are particularly keen exponents of shared values. For example, in 2008, Bill Rammell, then Minister for Further and Higher Education, had this to say:

> Our shared values which bind communities together belong to everyone in Britain; they are not possessed by one creed, race or nationality. The Further Education sector's task is to foster these values in their institutions...Colleges have a unique role to play in fostering our shared values of openness, free debate and tolerance.[1]

At Key Stage 3 in England, citizenship education is said to include engagement with "the values we share as citizens of the UK".[2] In like vein, the following appeared in the guidance document for schools on their statutory duty to promote community cohesion from September 2007:

> As a starting point, schools build community cohesion by promoting equality of opportunity and inclusion for different groups of pupils within a school. But alongside this focus on inequalities and a strong respect for diversity, they also have a role in promoting shared values and encouraging their pupils to actively engage with others to understand what they all hold in common.[3]

What exactly are these shared values? The suspicion is that they are thought to be self-evident commonsense. The only time that government has made a considered attempt to define a list for English schools was in 1996 when a diverse group of community leaders was brought together to form the National Forum on Values. It identified four areas in which values are important; the self, relationships, society and the environment. A list of agreed values emerged under each heading through an extensive consultation process and was subsequently appended to the National Curriculum.[4] The propagation of these values by the State through schools was considered justified on the grounds that they reflected a consensus that existed in society and which had been laid bare by the extensive consultation process. These still underpin the National Curriculum in force at the time of writing.[5]

An interesting variation on the theme of shared values is their interpretation as encapsulating the duties of citizenship. This emerged as a particular emphasis in the recent Labour government, such as in the then chancellor Gordon Brown's speech on "British-ness" delivered early in 2006 in response to the London bombings committed by young British citizens in July 2005.[6] He expressed British-ness in terms of common purpose. In 2007 this aspiration became linked to education with the call by the then Education Secretary Alan Johnson for schools to make more of "British values" following Sir Keith Ajegbo's influential report on citizenship.[7] In the latest guidance on RE for schools in England, the ideas of shared values and democratic values are used interchangeably, suggesting that they are assumed to describe the same set of values that schools should promote.[8] However, there is no developed statement of what these "shared/British/democratic" values are.

In Scotland the four values on which the curriculum is based are identified as "wisdom, justice, compassion and integrity". These were, seemingly, selected because they are inscribed on the mace of the Scottish Parliament. On the official curriculum website, it is stated:

> These words have helped define values for Scottish society, and should help young people in Scotland define their own position on matters of social justice and personal and collective responsibility.[9]

Since it is stated that the curriculum "must be inclusive", the assumption appears to be that these civic values provide an uncontroversial basis for inclusivity. Presumably that means they too are "shared values", which can, in all fairness, be insisted upon. But the rationale is not developed. It seems it is assumed to be clear.

These examples raise an important question as to exactly what people mean by shared values. *Do they mean values that people do share as a matter of fact or values that people think others ought to share because they are clearly objective?* The suspicion is that proponents of shared values might identify with Richard Norman when, towards the end of his book *On Humanism,* he commented:

> Looking back on the previous chapters, I cannot escape the feeling that everything I have said is obvious...I am also inclined to think that the broad position which I have defended is largely a matter of commonsense.[10]

The problem comes when there is a slide from assuming that shared values are uncontroversial *because people do in fact share them* to assuming that shared values are uncontroversial so that people ought to share them *because they are "obvious commonsense".* Where this happens there is a slide from fairness being respected by insistence on these values to the unfair imposition of these values in the name of purported fairness based on a misplaced sense of objectivity.

The difficulty with relying on shared values as the key to *both* objectivity and fairness can be illustrated by an example from the National Forum for Values in 1996 in England. In the original report, under the heading *Society,* it was stated that: "In particular, we value families as sources of love and support for all their members and as the basis of a society in which people care for others". Exemplifying this, the institution of marriage was picked out as particularly to be supported "whilst recognizing that love and commitment for a secure and happy childhood can be found in families of different kinds". In a revised version attached to a later version of the National Curriculum, the heading became the *diversity in our society,* the reference to marriage as particularly valued disappeared and the statement "we value families" was qualified by the phrase "including families of different kinds". The shift from privileging marriage as the ideal family to privileging diversity of family type reflects an ongoing debate in British society between those holding significantly different beliefs about what constitutes a family and the status of marriage. Even though there is clearly a shared value around the importance of family life, there is significant difference as to how that shared value should be interpreted. This difference has its roots in the very different beliefs held by different groups. Shared values can in fact be quite controversial depending on how they are interpreted!

> *Even though there is a shared value around the importance of family life, there is significant difference as to how that should be interpreted.*

The importance of interpretation is illustrated by the website launched by the Church of England which is designed to support Church schools in the development of their values.[11] In the list of values selected are many that would be welcomed by non-church schools, for example thankfulness, endurance and compassion. However, others would probably raise an eyebrow, including creation, wisdom and humility. The big surprise in the Church of England pack is *koinonia,* a word that would mean nothing to most teachers. It is defined as "that which is in common and is often translated as fellowship" and describes "the quality of relationship within the Christian community", the foundation of which is "Christ's self giving on the cross". But why not simply use a word like "interdependence" which would be more widely understood and not encumbered with Christian language? The reason is that the Church wants to make clear how Church schools should express their distinctively Christian character through giving the widely shared value of interdependence a particular interpretation based on Christian beliefs about its nature.

Does this mean that the Church is adding religious "clutter" to a shared value? Not so. The reality is that every shared value has to be interpreted on the basis of particular beliefs. In a non-religious school these interpretations will often be derived from humanist beliefs about what it means to be human, which the BHA claims are widely held by the silent majority. In schools with a religious character there will, or should, be a different understanding. What is important about shared values in education is not some bland assertion that, for example, kindness is a good thing, but the interpretation and application of kindness in different situations. Pupils need to grapple with what a value might mean in everyday life, what motivates people to live by their values, where values come from and so on. As the earlier family life example showed, this cannot happen without taking seriously the supposed "clutter" of contentious beliefs which cause people to view the same shared value in very different ways . Of course, someone might want to argue that religion-less "clutter" is objective when religious "clutter" is not, but that is to claim a status for secular beliefs which is unfair.

The implication of this discussion is that *values education must go hand in hand with beliefs education*. This will help pupils to understand and explore the foundations, interpretation and motivation for keeping different values and their dependency on beliefs. To assume that shared values stand on their own and that beliefs are "clutter" will result in the imposition of certain interpretations, usually secular in today's society, which are assumed to be "commonsense".

faith, belief and knowledge

In chapter 1, it was argued that much of the resistance to "doing God" in education is based on a belief that human knowledge and rationality are objective and therefore independent of the "clutter" of religious beliefs. The popularity of the discourse of shared values in current educational thinking reflects the influence of that position. The assumption appears to be that shared values are somehow universal because they are independent of the "clutter" of particular and controversial religious beliefs. The problem with this position is its dependence on the particular humanist belief that religion is "clutter" when it comes to knowledge. It is not therefore fair or inclusive to base public education on this approach because it unjustifiably privileges a secular view of knowledge. The important question then is, "is there an alternative understanding of the relationship between religious belief and human knowledge that will avoid these problems?"

The film *The Truman Show* may help. Released in 1998, it tells the story of Truman Burbank, a happily married insurance salesman living an idyllic life in small-town America. What he doesn't realize is that his world is the construction of a media company that had created the ultimate reality TV show around his life from the time he was a baby. Everyone in Truman's life, except him, is an actor. However, his suspicions are aroused by what he perceives as odd behaviour on the part of "his wife" when she engages in product placement advertising. They are confirmed later when a stage light drops and smashes perilously close to him. The rest of the film is the story of how Truman breaks out of this constructed world and makes contact with the "real, objective world" beyond the set. Truman's experience provides a helpful metaphor for exploring the relation between beliefs and knowledge. (Although, as with every metaphor, there are shortcomings. In this case it is the manipulative behaviour of the production team and fellow actors in constructing Truman's world around him. This is not intended to be part of the metaphor here.)

The position taken on the legitimacy of "doing God" in education is fundamentally shaped by people's understanding of the relationship between knowledge and the interpretations of that knowledge derived from their beliefs. There are, at least, four significant views to be taken into account. They can each be related to a particular perspective on *The Truman Show*.

1. Humanists in the Hirstian tradition probably would regard themselves as akin to the viewers of the show. They watch the weekly episode knowing that Truman himself is unconsciously trapped inside a world that is made up by other people. They believe that the best thing is to enable him to escape from the fiction in which he is trapped and which has been created by the interpretations of others, by helping him to see that there is an objective world to be discovered. Maybe one of them deliberately knocked the light to fall at Truman's feet? Ultimately they believe that true education would liberate Truman and release him from the "clutter" of the production company's storyline. Education is then the process of liberation from the shackles of other people's interpretations. This, broadly speaking, is the objectivist view advanced by Richard Norman.

2. In stark contrast to the objectivist position is that advanced by those who are very influenced by post-modern thinking but who are against indoctrination. They would agree that we are all, like Truman Burbank, born trapped inside a world constructed by other people. Applying this to human knowledge they would argue that knowledge is therefore always someone's interpretation and is shaped by the particular "belief clutter" out of which it has been constructed. The world outside of Truman's immediate experience is, as far as they are concerned, irrelevant. We can never access it. For them, the important thing is to be autonomous; in other words to have constructed one's own knowledge and one's own reality, to have chosen one's interpretation for oneself, to have made one's

own "clutter". Their view of education would be to help Truman take charge of the set on which he finds himself and to begin to construct his own storyline rather than have it imposed on him.

The influential religious educator Michael Grimmitt expresses a version of this view when he writes "in a world in which life-styles are often pre-packaged we should seek every opportunity to strengthen young people's capacity to 'roll their own'".[12] In similar vein, a philosophy for teenagers publication purportedly urged teachers to assist students in rejecting parental values in the cause of helping them to explore the identities and beliefs they want to "assume for themselves".[13] This view, called radical constructivism in the trade, is an influential alternative to the objectivist position. The problem with it is that it sinks into relativism in its denial of objectivity and truth.

3.   In reaction against this, some religious believers take the opposite view and align themselves with the media company featured in *The Truman Show*. Arguing that the objectivist view amounts to indoctrination into atheism, and the constructivist view indoctrination into relativism, they claim the right to induct pupils into their own religious understanding of the world. The problem with this view is that it turns education into a power struggle for dominance of schools' ethos and curriculum by one's own ideology. It is difficult to see how this can itself avoid the charges of indoctrination and tribalism and offers little hope for education being a force for community cohesion and well-being.

4.   The fourth position acknowledges the inevitable place of beliefs and construction in human knowledge, but does not see that as completely limiting access to objective reality in the way positions two and three do. This stance accepts that everyone grows up shaped by a particular view of the world held by their family and others of significance (including their school). But, as Truman Burbank experienced, it is maintained that *one can connect with objective reality from within one's own worldview* and that this can change one's perception. Learning, they believe, is the slow and painstaking process of constructing one's own interpretation of the world, shaped as it is by one's background, through encounters with reality and with people of other worldviews. In this way one becomes autonomous as one actively participates in constructing one's own interpretation of the world, so that it is more and more shaped by reality.

In this view, the so-called "clutter" of beliefs is integral to knowing, but our "clutter" is modified and develops as we learn. Education should, then, be a process where we each learn to reflect on the interpretations we make and the beliefs we hold as we construct our own understanding of the meaning and purpose of life.[14] This position is commonly known as critical realism. It puts beliefs and the worldviews they constitute at the heart of education. Judging from the storyline, it looks as though the makers of the Truman Show were probably critical realists. They portrayed the attempt of the reality show producers to restrict Truman's vision of the world to that which they constructed for him as not worthy of the name education.

Rather like *The Truman Show,* the argument of this essay will be that we each exist, to some degree, in a world constructed by the interpretations of our families, our schools and other significant people in our lives. This is an inescapable part of being human. For each of us, our teachers are like the reality TV show production company. They teach us facts and shared values, but they inevitably do that from within the context of certain interpretations which are derived from their own particular beliefs about what it means to be human. However, unlike the reality TV show production company, teachers should be actively encouraging their students to explore other interpretations and to come to their own conclusions about meaning and purpose in life. In the end, we are each accountable for our own decisions on this. It will not be adequate to rely solely on the interpretations others have constructed for us.

> *Humanists and Christians need to recognize each other's beliefs as integral to the development of their own interpretation of science.*

This four-fold classification is a gross over-simplification of a complex issue. However, it highlights the key influences on the educational debate about the legitimacy of "doing God". We have observed the influence of those who want to rid education of religious "clutter". The only alternatives that honour the significance of religious beliefs seem to be the sectarianism of position three or the relativism of position two. This is an unnecessarily pessimistic picture. Position four gives the opportunity for religious and non-religious believers to cooperate together in public education in a way that promotes inclusive education (by which people generally mean fair or non-discriminatory), whilst still allowing for "doing God".

What this might look like can be illustrated by considering again the debate between Francis Collins and Richard Dawkins outlined in chapter 1. The debate is too easily interpreted as a stand-off between atheists and Christians. Judging from the disparaging reviews that can be found of Collins' work on the worldwide web, much humanist thinking seems to be that Collins is irrational in his interpretation of genetics whereas Dawkins is rational. This is not a recipe for an inclusive approach to education in which those of religious belief feel that they are taken seriously. Likewise Christian rejection of Dawkins' atheism as "rebellion against God" will also fall short of being an inclusive approach.

To move education towards a position that is compatible with position four, I suggest humanists and Christians need to recognize each other's beliefs as integral to the development of their own interpretation of science. (That is not, incidentally, the same as recognizing the correctness of someone else's view.) The place that Collins' Christian beliefs and Dawkins' atheist beliefs play in their respective understandings of the meaning and purpose of science both need to receive serious attention, rather than Dawkins' view being privileged and Collins' dismissed as "clutter" as is suggested in the objectivist view, or vice-versa as in some Christian education approaches. Children should be taught to understand both views, and to evaluate them for themselves in their own pursuit of understanding the truth about reality. They should be taught the skill of making judgments about the truth of different interpretations as the means to discovering the meaning and significance of what they are learning about for themselves. But no-one can escape the fact that such an education will inevitably take place from within a worldview perspective.

The challenge for those advocating an objectivist view is to accept that religious beliefs are not "clutter", which implies *irrelevance* to knowledge and seems to be the major reason for their opposition to "doing God" in education. There will also need to be a change in how they regard their own beliefs. At present atheists appear to see them as rational or neutral in stark contrast to the "clutter" of religious beliefs. But it is difficult to see how this insistence on secular beliefs shaping the understanding of education is inclusive or fair.

nurture and autonomy

Autonomy is an important theme that permeates debates about the place of religion in education. Its antithesis is presumed to be nurture, where children are brought up in the beliefs of a particular community. The nurture/autonomy debate provides a case study of how a shift to position four changes our understanding of education.

It has been argued that there is confusion as to whether, when they talk about autonomy, people mean children choosing for themselves or choosing in a way that is objective, in other words uninfluenced by the "clutter" of religious beliefs. The rhetoric usually implies the former when in reality the latter is the aspiration.

The BHA billboard campaign of November 2009 illustrates this point. This has pictures of happy children with the caption: "Please don't label me. Let me grow up and choose for myself".[17] The campaign was launched by Richard Dawkins whose views on religious nurture are understood to mirror the message of the campaign. In *The God Delusion,* Dawkins rejects children being labelled with the faith of their parents. "That is not a Muslim child, but a child of Muslim parents."[18] He goes on to say: "The very sound of the phrase 'Christian child' or 'Muslim child' should grate like fingernails on a board."[19] This clearly expresses a concern that children should make their own decisions as to the beliefs that will shape their life, that they should not feel this is pre-determined by the accident of their birth. This sounds eminently reasonable.

But Dawkins is concerned about much more. He later goes on to say that: "Small children are too young to decide their views on the origins of the cosmos, of life and of morals…let them make up their own minds when they are old enough."[20] In a lecture to the American Humanist Association, he described nurturing a child in a religious faith as

> *Dawkins' ideal is to offer children an upbringing that is free from religious "clutter".*

"mental child abuse".[21] Dawkins' ideal is to offer children an upbringing that is free from religious "clutter" until they are old enough to decide for themselves. In his view, that is the only way that rational and autonomous choices can be made. His expectation is that no-one will choose a religious way of life in those circumstances. This is clearly an example of the objectivist position (Position 1 above).

It is therefore interesting to note that humanists run their own summer camps called Camp Quest. The description of them is:

> CQUK is the first residential summer camp for the children of atheists, agnostics, humanists, freethinkers and all those who embrace a naturalistic rather than supernatural world view…Children at Camp Quest aren't "required" to be atheists. We want to encourage children to think for themselves and to evaluate the world critically and thus draw their own conclusions. However, parents should be aware that we adopt a critical, scientific approach as opposed to a "faith-based" approach. At Camp Quest, children *aren't* taught that "There is no god". Instead, they are taught to come to their own conclusions, but more importantly, that "It's OK not to believe in a god".[22]

The theme of the first ever British Camp Quest in 2009 was evolution. One of the much heralded activities was the invisible unicorn challenge described as follows:

> Every Camp Quest is inhabited by no less and no more than two invisible unicorns. These unicorns can't hurt you, don't eat anything and, in general, leave no trace and keep themselves to themselves. It is up to the campers to disprove the existence of these unicorns. The first camper to prove that the unicorns don't exist will receive a ten pound note (and if the approving face of Charles Darwin wasn't enough!) signed by famous scientist and writer Richard Dawkins. The American prize is a hundred dollar bill without the inscription "In God we Trust". To this date, no camper has completed the challenge.

> Our unicorns are very misunderstood and have filed complaints to the ethical standards department of several tabloid newspapers. Unfortunately, neither can be seen, heard, smelled, touched or tasted. All the camp counselors have faith that the unicorns exist and find words like "onus" and "fallacy" deeply offensive. Their beliefs are proven by years of tradition and proclamations of fact from some very important people.

But unicorns are mysterious things and sometimes something very strange happens: Many of the campers…build an appreciation and understanding of the unicorns in the very process of disproving their existence. These campers help the rest of us carry on the conversation.[23]

This camp activity, designed to produce "free-thinkers", is as clear an example of nurture into a particular understanding of the world as would be encountered on similar activities run by religious communities. The assumption of an atheist framework is justified on the grounds that it is not "faith-based".[24] But it is clearly designed to persuade campers that invisible unicorns (like God) do not exist.

There is nothing wrong with camps that are designed to nurture children in the parental worldview. What is unhelpful, however, is for "free-thinkers" to assume that nurture into atheist beliefs is rational and ethical, offering no threat of indoctrination, whereas nurture into religious beliefs is mental child abuse.

> *The idea that free-thinkers have not been nurtured by their background is simply wrong.*

If human knowledge is constructed from within a belief framework, as the critical realist position four maintains, then it is clearly both inevitable and essential that children are nurtured into a worldview from the earliest age. Without this experience children cannot think at all. On this view, free-thinkers are people, be they atheists or religious believers, who have learnt to examine and reflect critically upon the worldview in which they have been nurtured. The idea that free-thinkers have not been nurtured by their background is simply wrong.

The Canadian philosopher Elmer Thiessen has introduced the concept of *normal rationality* into debates about the place of religion in education.[25] Normal rationality is meant to highlight the fact that nurture into belief and tradition are part and parcel of becoming a rational thinker. Autonomy is achieved by growing through a worldview, not by never experiencing one until old enough to choose for oneself. Children from atheist families and children from religious families face exactly the same challenge in life. They need to be nurtured in a worldview in a manner that enables them to think for themselves as they grow into adulthood. The assumption that autonomy cannot be achieved when education is "doing God" is based on the belief that rationality can only be achieved independently of "religious clutter". This assumption elevates the humanist understanding of knowledge to a privileged position in public education rather than promoting autonomy. It will not promote fairness since it means children from religious families will only have the option of a humanist-shaped education.

conclusion

So far this report has argued that the influential approach that treats religious beliefs as irrelevant clutter in education is unhelpful, both because it is unfair (chapter 1) and because it is a misunderstanding of the nature of human knowledge (chapter 2). It has been suggested that the opposite is true, namely that beliefs, including religious beliefs, are integral to human knowing and therefore education. The next two chapters will explore the positive implications of this conclusion, examining what difference it makes in practice (chapter 3) and how schools can still be inclusive and fair places when seeking to embrace the diversity of religious and non-religious communities that make up Britain today (chapter 4).

chapter 2 references

1. Speech on 11 February 2008. See http://www.dius.gov.uk/news_and_speeches/press_releases/college_change.

2. See http://curriculum.qca.org.uk/key-stages-3-and-4/subjects/key-stage-3/citizenship/programme-of-study/index.aspx .

3. DCSF *Guidance on the duty to promote community cohesion* (2007), p. 7. See http://www.teachernet.gov.uk/_doc/11635/Guidance%20on%20the%20duty%20to%20promote %20community %20cohesion%20pdf.pdf .

4. See http://curriculum.qcda.gov.uk/uploads/Statement-of-values_tcm8-12166.pdf.

5. See http://curriculum.qcda.gov.uk/key-stages-1-and-2/Values-aims-and-purposes/index.aspx.

6. See Stephen Backhouse, *Red, White, Blue … and Brown* (Theos, 2007) for further discussion.

7. http://news.bbc.co.uk/1/hi/education/6294643.stm. Sir Keith Ajegbo, *Diversity and Citizenship,* (Department for Education and Skills, 2007) http://publications.teachernet.gov.uk/eOrderingDownload/DfES_Diversity_&_Citizenship.pdf.

8. *Religious education in English schools: Non-statutory guidance 2010,* (Department for Children, Schools and Families, 2010) pp. 7-8.

9. http://www.ltscotland.org.uk/curriculumforexcellence/curriculumoverview/aims/index.asp.

10. Norman, *On Humanism,* p. 132.

11. See http://www.christianvalues4schools.co.uk/.

12. Michael Grimmitt, *Religious Education and Human Development* (McCrimmons, 1987) p. 208.

13. Adi Bloom, "Don't forget to rebel: advice to teens" in *Times Educational Supplement,* 8 January 2010, p. 6. See http://www.tes.co.uk/Article.aspx?storycode=6032767.

14. See Trevor Cooling, "Curiosity: Vice or Virtue for the Christian Teacher?" in *Journal of Education & Christian Belief,* 9.2, (2005) pp. 87-104 for further discussion of this position. NT Wright and Professor Alister McGrath are influential Christian theologians who adopt this view.

15. For further discussion of the relationship of religious belief and knowledge see, for example, Trevor Cooling, *A Christian Vision for State Education* (SPCK, 1994), Trevor Hart, *Faith Thinking* (SPCK, 1995), Richard Middleton & Brian Walsh, *Truth is Stranger than it Used to Be* (SPCK, 1995), Alister McGrath, *A Scientific Theology: volumes 1-3* (T&T Clark, 2001-2003), Andrew Wright, *Religion, Education and Post-modernity* (RoutledgeFalmer, 2004), Michael Goheen & Craig Bartholomew, *Living at the Crossroads* (SPCK, 2008), Andrew Wright, *Critical religious education, multiculturalism and the pursuit of truth* (University of Wales Press,2007).

16. Professor Anthony Thiselton calls this "pre-understanding" in his *Hermeneutics: An Introduction* (Eerdmans, 2009), chapter 1.

17. http://www.humanism.org.uk/billboards.

18. Dawkins, *The God Delusion,* p. 25.

19. Ibid, p. 381.

20. Ibid, p. 381-83.

21. Richard Dawkins, "Is science a Religion?" in *The Humanist,* (January/February 1997), http://www.thehumanist.org/humanist/articles/dawkins.html.

21. http://www.camp-quest.org.uk/welcome/welcome-to-camp-quest/.

23. http://www.camp-quest.org.uk/activities/.

24. See Stephen Law, "What's so wrong with faith?" (2002) for an exposition of humanist concerns about the concept of faith (http://www.humanism.org.uk/about/philosophers/faq/whats-so-wrong-with-faith).

25. See Elmer John Thiessen, *Teaching for Commitment* (Gracewing, 1993).

doing God in education:
what difference does it make?

What, then, might "doing God" in education actually look like? Paul Hirst's scepticism that this is a legitimate aspiration was noted in chapter 1. He would no doubt have shared the incredulity expressed by the person who, on hearing the suggestion that there is a distinctively Christian way to teach modern foreign languages, asked "is there a Christian way to boil water?"[1] This chapter will present an alternative understanding to the influential concept of neutral education, arguing that there may indeed be a Christian way "to boil water". It will use the teaching of modern foreign languages as an extended case study on the grounds that this is generally seen as a skills-based subject where neutral grammar and vocabulary are taught and should therefore be independent of religious beliefs.

Central to the argument will be the point derived from the example of Richard Dawkins and Francis Collins discussed at the start of the essay. Although information, theories, disciplinary methods and skills may indeed be common to human knowledge and shared by people irrespective of their worldview, the *interpretation* of the meaning and significance and the *application in life* of these will be *dependent* on the worldview held. That worldview may be religious or non-religious, consciously held or a sub-conscious influence, but it will frame the way in which the knowledge learnt is understood.

The optical illusions beloved of perceptual psychologists are a simple illustration of the point. Take for example the famous young woman/old woman illusion. Everyone looking at this "sees" exactly the same lines on a page in the sense that the image on each of their retinas is the same. But what they interpret those lines as meaning is often different. Some will perceive them as a young woman, some will perceive them as an old woman and some will perceive both. Usually a lively debate will erupt between advocates of the different interpretations when this picture is shown to a group. It is not the shared information of the lines on the page that generates interest; rather it is what these are *interpreted* to mean that people want to debate.

The pivotal argument of this report is this: in human life it is the interpretations of the meaning and significance, and the applications made, of shared knowledge and values that ultimately matter. It is these that inspire people, not the shared information that they learn. They shape the sorts of adults that pupils become. Education should not, therefore, just be about passing on knowledge and skills. Rather it should strive to support people

39

in the process of making their own wholesome interpretations of human knowledge and of applying those in their lives. That means it should help them to reflect on and evaluate the significance of their worldview in the growth of human understanding and to deal with the fact that people disagree when making interpretations. To achieve this, beliefs must be treated as integral, not "clutter".

> **Education is always based on a vision of what it means to flourish as a human being.**

Education is always based on a vision of what it means to flourish as a human being. This vision will be derived from a worldview. The arguments against "doing God" in education are based on discrimination against religious worldviews on the grounds that they import irrelevant and potentially harmful clutter. It has already been argued that this is unfair. The rest of this chapter offers a second challenge by exploring what the impact of designing education on the basis of a distinctively Christian vision of human flourishing might be.

the case of modern foreign languages

The research of David I Smith and Barbara Carvill, two academics working on the connection between Christian belief and the teaching of modern foreign languages (MFL) will serve as a case study. Their focal question is, "What difference does it make to the way we teach if we, as Christians, think of our students as primarily spiritual beings and if we see MFL teaching as contributing to their spiritual development?"[2] The proposal of this report is that if it can be shown that there is a distinctively Christian approach to teaching as fact- and skills-based a subject as MFL, then it can legitimately be assumed that there is a distinctive Christian contribution to all other subjects.

Carvill describes a revelatory moment in her professional life as an MFL teacher which took place in China.[3] She was on an excursion with a group of American teachers when their bus met a tractor driven by a young Chinese man and loaded with hay bales. He attempted to squeeze through the narrow gap beside the bus, but misjudged the manoeuvre and the bales smashed the windows and showered the teachers in the bus with shards of glass. Mercifully, there were no serious injuries, but the young man was apprehended by locals and made to walk past the Americans to survey the distress he had caused. He was mortified. In the end Carvill, as the group leader, was asked to go and speak to him and reassure him that the Americans had forgiven him. He needed to hear it from her in his own language. It was at that point that Carvill realized that her languages education had not prepared her for this type of relational interaction. Her Chinese phrase book did not include an entry for forgiving someone. Had she needed to apologize to him, to complain about the service he offered, to purchase something from him, to ask directions, the appropriate phrase was available. But it apparently had never crossed the compilers' minds that their end user might need to forgive someone.

Carvill notes that the incident taught her something about cultural differences between the Chinese and Americans when it comes to road traffic accidents. Her first reaction was to reach for the insurance documents, not to plan an act of confession and absolution. More significantly, it also made her question American approaches to MFL. She realized that the way in which it was taught made certain relationships between the language learner and the native language speaker normative, for example consumer and provider of services, whilst it ignored others, such as wronged and wrongdoer. Are there, she wondered, implicit messages that are being conveyed about meaning and significance of the human interaction we call language in current approaches to MFL teaching? What difference would it make if it focused consciously on promoting the spiritual character of the learner?

As an example Carvill describes a German oral exercise where students were asked to assume that someone had given them a million dollars.[4] The exercise required them to talk about what they would spend it on. Carvill realized that this exercise was reinforcing the prevailing assumption that the purpose of having money is consumption. So she changed the exercise, asking students to talk about how they would give away the money and what good ends they would hope to achieve by this. One student "felt that the wording of my question manipulated him into doing more good than he was capable of." The MFL exercise had made the student think about deeper issues than German grammar and vocabulary, namely his attitude to financial generosity. But none of the students felt manipulated by the previous exercise which had asked them to spend the money on themselves! Carvill's new approach disturbed the comfort of the students' taken-for-granted approach to life. This is MFL teaching that regards the educational outcome not simply as learning how to speak a language, but also as students learning something about themselves as spiritual persons. It means that the professional concern of the teacher is not just with the technical competence of the students as linguists, but with the sort of person that they are now and will develop into in the future.

Carvill and Smith go on to argue that underpinning different approaches to MFL teaching are different conceptions of language learners that define the relationship between learner and native speaker.[5] These included the entrepreneur (to grasp new economic opportunities), the persuader (to gain advantage in the foreign culture) and the connoisseur (self-improvement through cross-cultural experience). A predominant model in many school textbooks was that of the learner as tourist, where:

> …the tourist's world is defined by immediate survival requirements, leisure activities and pragmatic transactions: paying for services, asking for directions, securing help in case of emergency, and the like. It is a world that is often virtually bereft of any spiritual experience.[6]

Carvill's and Smith's conclusion is that MFL teaching cannot escape adopting a framework which implicitly or explicitly defines the relationship of the learner and the native speaker. This, in turn, rests on certain understandings of what matters about being human. These assumptions are conveyed through the exercises that are set and the contexts in which the language itself is studied. Their conclusion is that students are thereby being inducted into a worldview through the way in which they are taught the supposedly "neutral" grammar and vocabulary of the particular language studied. In their view, in western education this largely reinforced the contemporary love affair with consumerist individualism.[7]

The next question for Carvill and Smith was how their Christian worldview might provide an alternative worldview framework for MFL teaching. They were certainly looking to achieve something far more significant than simply adding blessed religious thoughts or Bible quotations to neutral lessons. They wanted to offer a distinctively Christian understanding of the relationship between the learner and the native speaker, in particular one that "developed concern for the speakers of the other language as *people, valuable in themselves*".[8] They therefore surveyed the resources of their Protestant Christian tradition with its particular emphasis on the teachings of the Bible and focused on the theme of hospitality to the stranger which encapsulated the biblical vision for "reconciliation, for justice and peace among nations" and is "shaped by respect for the other as image bearer of God".[9] In the light of this they proposed that *"foreign language education prepare students for two related callings: to be a blessing as strangers in a foreign land and to be hospitable to strangers in their own homeland"*.[10] Hospitality to the stranger therefore acts as "a metaphor for the way both teachers and students understand and interact with otherness", where otherness is understood as the encounter with the native speaker of the language being learnt.[11] They describe this as *xenophilic hospitality* and distinguish it from *diaconal hospitality*, which, in the tradition of the Good Samaritan story focuses on meeting the needs of the "stranger in distress".[12] Xenophilic hospitality, rather, focuses on the need to welcome a stranger from another nation or culture because he or she is an image bearer of Christ.

> With this kind of hospitality we graciously invite a foreign guest, a foreign tongue, foreign ways into our homes, lives, minds and hearts…Our goal should be to nurture students in such a way that they look forward with openness and curiosity to strangers, and joyfully welcome the enrichment and change their visits bring for both hosts and guests.[13]

Carvill and Smith summarize their approach by highlighting the three basic questions that it leads them to ask as Christians when evaluating the different approaches to MFL teaching.

1. What kinds of persons do the proponents of the different approaches want their students to become?

2.   What kinds of relationships to native speakers do these different approaches nurture?

3.   To what degree does any given approach honour the stranger as one created in God's image, "as one who hopes thinks, suffers, trusts, and weeps and whose sighs and laughter are just as audible to God as our own"?[14]

For Carvill and Smith the role of their distinctively Christian contribution to MFL teaching is to challenge the "time-honoured human habit of dividing the world into members of our culture on the one hand, and lesser beings of inferior importance on the other".[15] The relevance of this approach in an educational climate where community cohesion is an urgent priority is obvious.[16]

A significant point now emerges. This is clearly a *distinctively Christian* approach because it is inspired by reflection on the teachings of the Christian tradition about what it means to flourish as a human being and has its origin in study of the Bible.[17] It arises out of Christian theological reflection on the way MFL is taught in the USA and UK. Sometimes this claim to distinctiveness is interpreted as implying that other religious and non-religious worldviews are therefore unable to generate similar insights. This is not the case; people of many other religious and non-religious worldviews would undoubtedly applaud this emphasis on the quality of relationships as challenging the prevailing consumerist and excessively individualist culture of modern western societies. Indeed, I am sure people from other worldviews could have reached similar conclusions, for example through distinctively Islamic or humanist reflection.

So the claim to be distinctively Christian by "doing God" in education is not the claim to be *exclusively different or superior*, but rather is highlighting the distinctive outcome of seeking to be faithful to Christian beliefs in the way one teaches MFL. This does not make the distinctive Christian contribution redundant, because it provides the theological foundations for educational insight. The problem with much education is that it offers children exhortation with no foundation, the what without the why, and therefore becomes moralizing. Furthermore, Smith and Carvill would not have generated their distinctive approach without first interrogating the Bible. Doing so led them to offer a very different approach to the prevailing professional consensus. The fact that their new approach is also highly persuasive to others merely highlights its professional excellence; it does not diminish its Christian authenticity. The work of Smith and Carvill thus underlines the importance of worldview in education in providing the framework within which the subjects taught are interpreted and applied. It therefore confronts the claim that education is a worldview-neutral activity.

This is hugely important. The neutral approach claims that religious worldviews are irrelevant, possibly toxic, "clutter" when it comes to education. In contrast, the argument for "doing God" is that worldviews are integral to educational policy and practice since they are the source of the underpinning vision for what it means to flourish as a human.

The objection to so-called neutral approaches, then, is that they privilege secular worldviews and are in danger of implicit anti-religious indoctrination. They are not, in other words, neutral. To argue for "doing God" is not to add irrelevant "clutter", nor is it to seek to privilege a religious worldview. Rather it is to request that the role of worldview in education in interpreting and applying knowledge is properly recognized. It is to ask that religious and non-religious worldviews are treated as *resources* to be tapped in the cause of pupil well-being and flourishing, not as *problems* to be confronted and marginalized. The aspiration to offer distinctively Christian education should not be perceived as a tribal threat but as an opportunity to enhance and enrich education in a worldview-diverse context by drawing on the resources of a constituent faith community.

> To argue for "doing God" is to ask that religious and non-religious worldviews are treated as resources to be tapped in the cause of pupil well-being and flourishing, not as problems to be confronted and marginalized.

These insights from MFL can be applied to all other subjects on the curriculum. What is required is a commitment on the part of curriculum planners to raise their sights from focusing on the question, "what has to be done to ensure that pupils become competent in the knowledge and skills inherent to my subject?" to addressing the question, "how can my subject be taught in a way that promotes the development of pupils as spiritual beings?" In other words the concern moves from purely focusing on subject competence to focusing on the contribution that can be made by subject teaching to character development. This requires, firstly, an awareness of the way in which current approaches may be promoting influential, but challengeable, values, attitudes and dispositions; secondly, a vision for alternative values, attitudes and dispositions inspired by Christian belief; and thirdly, a clear idea of how promoting these would make a difference to teaching. Two brief examples will illustrate the point.

The maths department in a church secondary school wanted to contribute to pupils' development of empathy. They reviewed the teaching of pie charts which currently comprised an exercise where pupils recorded the main activities of their own day and created a pie chart to give them a means of analyzing the data collected. The teachers asked themselves "what if we taught pie charts to encourage empathy so as to help to move the pupils from a focus on self to an awareness of others' needs?" Their strategy was to amend the exercise so that pupils now used data from their mother's or main carer's day. They then gave pupils the data from recording the activities in the day of a mother in an African village. As well as learning how to construct pie charts, the pupils were also encouraged to reflect on the time their mother or carer gave to looking after them and the challenge of daily life for people with less privileged life-styles, rather than just focus on themselves. This approach tackles the question "what if maths was taught so as to promote gratitude and empathy?"[18]

A church primary school wanted to help its pupils move on from the feeling that "life owed you good outcomes". They felt this was an unhealthy feature of life in western society and that people in less privileged contexts were much more adjusted to making the most of life whatever their experience. As Christians they felt that learning to accept that life cannot always "go our way" and relying instead on a deeper sense of significance derived from a Christian understanding of hope in God was a message that should be conveyed in school. They asked themselves the question, "what if we taught football in PE in a way that encouraged greater acceptance of unfairness than is currently prevalent?" They had identified that the relationship between referees and professional players prevalent in football culture reinforced a sense that you were always entitled to fair treatment and could abuse another person if they ever failed to deliver that. During the course of a term pupils played five-a-side games where they experienced being player, linesman and referee. At the end of the term they discussed their experience of these roles and then watched videos of professional games. A key question was "how does it feel to be a referee and how can players respond to referees' decisions in ways that respect them as people created in God's image?" The aim was to promote a more magnanimous approach based on the importance of respecting the referee's dignity as a human being.

It is not expected that every reader will agree with or like these approaches. That is not the reason for recounting them. Rather what they are intended to show is that every subject contributes to pupils' development as people. Either this can happen "beneath the radar" or the teacher can consciously address the issue. The examples illustrate that teaching and learning will be different if conscious attention is given to a subject's impact on the values, attitudes and dispositions developed by pupils. Religious beliefs contribute to this process by guiding decisions as to the values, attitudes and dispositions that it is desirable to promote. They are not just "clutter".[19]

the importance of content and method

Adopting the approach advocated by Carvill and Smith has implications for both content and method in the classroom. This can be illustrated by two examples that Smith has developed.

His reflections on content relate to the teaching of German grammar.[20] Commenting on one particular textbook, he finds little wrong except that it presents a narrow, even trivial, view of the life of German people. Herr Roth sold his shares, Herr Zimmler received a cheque, the Baumanns have gone on holiday and Kurt drove his car too fast.

As an alternative Smith developed a series of grammar exercises based around the life of Adaline Kelbert, an unknown Hamburg housewife who was a friend of a friend of his.[21] Born near Kiev in 1903 into a German speaking family, Kelbert's life was marked by disruption and suffering. During the First World War she lived as a refugee dependent on the hospitality of other families. Between the wars she was persecuted by the communists. Her home was taken and her new husband was imprisoned. The Second World War was just as traumatic. As German speakers her family was deported to Germany and her husband and two sons were conscripted into the German army; tragically the younger son never returned. The family then settled permanently near Hamburg. Adaline Kelbert's feelings about her experience of life reflect a spiritual dimension for students to ponder.

In his adaptation of the story for the classroom, Smith used photographs of the family's life to stimulate oral work with pupils. This was interspersed with reading and listening activities where pupils used their knowledge of German grammar and vocabulary to interact with the life experience of this previously unknown but remarkable "real person".

> I remind students periodically that the reason we need to step aside and work on specific language points, including the formation of the past tense, is that if we do not, we risk misunderstanding and thus disrespecting what she has to tell us. Grammar can serve respect, and not merely grades, and learning a new language is as much about acquiring the humility needed to *hear* voices well that were previously marginal to us as it is about enhancing our abilities to *speak* in our own voices.[22]

Smith's hope is to overcome the impression, given by so many textbooks, that native speakers are cardboard cut-outs, stereotypes with very restricted lives. Here was someone who exemplified spiritual resilience in the midst of awful experiences. The reason for learning grammar is so that we can *listen effectively to her voice*. This mode of study leads to discussions in German about where this resilience came from and language exercises that engage with the spiritual and moral dimensions of a life where "faith" was a natural part of the everyday. Her experience of hospitality received at the hands of a poor Tartar family, her perception that milk and bread were luxuries in the dark days of World War I and a family photograph in her front room when she was in her nineties all give pupils the opportunity to link language learning with reflection on spiritual and moral issues.

> Then I ask what is most important to Adaline, aged 93 at this point? The inevitable answer is: people. There are many photos, but none show cars or other possessions, scenery or tourist destinations. This invites a further question. If people are likely to be the most important thing to you if you live to be 93, does that affect what you value now? Does it suggest any grounds for reflection on the choices you will make and the priorities you will set between now and then?[23]

Having studied Adaline Kelbert's life, students then interview an older person known to them with a view to "hearing" their life story and communicating it to the rest of the group using their knowledge of the German language. The ultimate aim of this work is not just that the students have learnt some technicalities of German grammar, gained new vocabulary and developed their linguistic skills (obviously all important objectives), but that they have also reflected on their own values, attitudes and behaviours and interacted with a native speaker in spiritually and morally significant ways. To adapt the language that is influential amongst those who teach religious education, *the students have not only learnt about German in class, but they have learnt something significant about themselves from their German lessons.*[24]

Turning to the way in which teaching method impacts students, Smith describes the development of a course for trainee teachers on literature from German speaking countries post-1945.[25] In particular, he highlights his frustration with the manner in which his students engaged with the prescribed texts in his early versions of the course. Their priority was mastery of the text with a view to performing well in assessment tasks. As a Christian teacher, his vision was that students should develop virtues like charity, humility and justice through seeking to hear the author in the best light, through being willing to listen carefully and learn from the author and through seeking to understand the author in his/her own terms before making critical judgment. Smith's observation was that the widely utilized practices of language teaching actually promoted attitudes and behaviours that were in opposition to these virtues by encouraging high-speed, superficial and selective reading. A distinctively Christian approach to reading a text would, he thought, encourage contrasting behaviour such as meditative, contextually aware and repeated reading of a text.

> *Students should develop virtues like charity, humility and justice.*

In his article, Smith describes a number of innovative revisions to his teaching method which were designed to influence the way that his students engaged with the prescribed texts. One innovation was the way he began the course. Smith's own words are quoted here at length in an attempt to capture the experience of his classroom.

> I came to class early and set up a looping PowerPoint presentation consisting entirely of black and white photos of rubble and extermination camps against a black background. I also set a piece of dissonant ambient music looping on the computer, and blacked out the classroom. Finally, I removed all the chairs and hung a sign at the door inviting students to enter in silence. Then I left and deliberately returned five minutes after the start of class. Fifteen students sat in silence on the floor; I sat down in the middle and said: "its 1945, we are in Germany, and you are a writer: what is it like?" One of the things that I immediately learned as my students proceeded to give me most of what had been in my lecture the year before was that one has a different kind of discussion with students when seated with them on the floor in the dark than when standing over their desks in a brightly lit classroom. In setting up the classroom the way I did I attempted to physically enact a posture of humility for our initial approach to the experience of

the Germans whom we were about to read, and to create a more affectively compelling pedagogical context that called for empathy. In doing so I hoped to take a step toward reframing my students' approach to the texts read during the semester.[26]

This specific approach is not one that could easily be copied by teachers in primary and secondary schools. But it illustrates a very important insight. The methods that teachers use convey messages as to the meaning and significance of the material being learnt. They shout at pupils with a vision of what it means to flourish as a human. Those messages can be changed by reflecting on a distinctively Christian understanding of the purpose of learning a subject. Teaching methods are not then neutral techniques simply to be assessed in terms of their effectiveness. Rather they convey worldviews, reflect values and promote virtues.

beyond MFL

This extended discussion of MFL, with the occasional foray into other subjects, demonstrates how a Christian worldview generates a distinctive approach to teaching and learning. It also illustrates how, whether we are aware of it or not, all teaching is shaped by and conveys worldview messages. In the sense that every classroom communicates a distinctive worldview, every teacher, from early years to university lecturer, is therefore "doing God" in their professional life. They are never just transmitting neutral knowledge.

It is beyond the scope of this essay to explore how this important insight will impact the rest of the curriculum. Certainly there is a dearth of support for classroom practitioners in understanding how worldview influences teaching and learning. However, to illustrate further the implications of "doing God" in education, the rest of this chapter will explore two areas of school life that particularly attract media attention because religious worldviews are involved.

the debate about creationism

We have already seen how Michael Reiss, an eminent science educator, was shipwrecked on the reef of creationism.[27] This issue seems to have become one of the litmus tests in the debates about the place of religious faith in education which followed the revelation that both the Principal and the Head of Science at Emmanuel School, Gateshead were purportedly creationists.[28] The school was one of the first of New Labour's new state schools to have a Christian sponsor in the form of Sir Peter Vardy and the press had a field day in suggesting, probably unfairly, that he had purchased the privilege of indoctrinating students into this view of origins through sponsoring the school. In response to the controversy, the Labour Government at the time published guidelines on how creationism was to be handled in schools.[29] Even Michael Gove, now Secretary of State for Education and keen to attract Christian groups to support the new "independent" schools championed by his party, made sure that he distanced himself from any suggestion that creationism would be taught in science lessons in these new schools.[30] To allow oneself to be accused of being a creationist is educational suicide.

The Government's guidance is that creationism should not be taught in science lessons since it is not a scientific theory. If pupils ask questions, teachers are advised to explain why creationism is not considered to be a scientific theory. That some religious believers are creationists can, however, be taught in religious education. This approach looks pretty reasonable given that virtually all scientists accept evolution as the best scientific explanation for the diversity of the natural world. It also seems fair in that it allows the minority voice of creationists, with their strong religious disposition, to have their views represented.

The danger, however, is that this advice strengthens the widely-held perception that science teaching is a neutral, rational activity where mention of religion would be irrelevant "clutter". The guidance does not intend to reinforce the idea that science and religion conflict, since the point is clearly made that many scientists believe in creation by God even though they don't believe in creationism. However, the probability is that in treating creationism in this way the idea that *any type of God-talk* is inappropriate in the science classroom is reinforced. We saw earlier how the fact that Michael Reiss was a clergyman was perceived by some very eminent scientists to be reason enough to remove him from his post as Education Officer at the Royal Society. The problem is that the Government guidance does not require science teachers to ensure that their pupils understand that every scientist practices his or her science within the context of a worldview, be that religious or not. Pupils are not generally sensitized to the importance of worldview through current approaches to science education. This is the reason why, in response to the publication of the government guidance, Justin Thacker, a qualified paediatric doctor with a PhD in theology writing on behalf of the Evangelical Alliance, decided to call himself a creationist when he is emphatically not a creationist.[31]

The clue to the problem lies in the Dawkins/Collins debate examined in the Introduction to this essay. The message of the guidance appears to be that science teaching is no more than transmission of the corroborated knowledge and skills of science and that any God-talk is therefore illegitimate. In this situation, discussion of the meaning and purpose of science has therefore to be set within a framework *where the absence of God is taken for granted*. In other words Dawkins' position becomes normative in the science classroom and Collins' position silenced, although it can be studied in RE lessons. Thacker, although welcoming the guidance, sums up the potential problem:

> The wider danger, here, is that science becomes cut off from other disciplines that are relevant. Science can only be properly understood or applied when it is put in its social, historical, philosophical, ethical and religious context. The history of

science has shown that there are serious dangers in isolating science from these other subjects, and we hope that this latest guidance will not increase the likelihood of this.

There are several unfortunate, but likely, consequences of this approach. Firstly, the current influence of scientism (the widespread idea that a religious view of the world is, at best, a tolerated private deviation and, at worst, an intellectual nonsense) will be reinforced. Putting it provocatively, science lessons might be seen as the place where you learn credible, established knowledge and RE the place where you study the myriad of "bonkers beliefs" to be found in the world. Secondly, the fact that there are many scientists who are committed Christians like Francis Collins is usually ignored. Thirdly, faith schools are prevented from setting their science teaching within the context of a distinctive worldview on the grounds that the atheistic worldview offers the only rational understanding of the relationship between science and belief. To return to an early theme, this is unfair discrimination against religious worldviews and amounts to indoctrination into humanism.

It is for this reason that Thacker called himself a creationist. Not in the sense that he is a biblical literalist but on the grounds that he wanted a Christian worldview to be taken seriously in education and recognized as a legitimate framework from within which to understand the meaning and purpose of science.

This can be done by following the lead of Smith and Carvill in MFL and asking the question, "what difference does it make to the way we teach if we, as Christians, think of our students as primarily spiritual beings and if we see science teaching as contributing to their spiritual development?"

the debate about school worship

Compulsory Christian worship for all pupils in school has been a characteristic feature of state education in the UK for as long as anyone can remember. Its origins lie in the pivotal role that the church played in the beginnings of universal education. By 1988, its position was highly controversial given the feeling on the part of many that such an activity being compulsory amounted to indoctrination and was a breach of human rights. The assumption that Christian worship and British citizenship went hand in hand was no longer tenable.

However, in 1988 attempts to revise the English and Welsh law to make school worship more acceptable ran aground in the House of Lords in the face of a concerted campaign to retain Christian worship. The resulting compromise was a complex theological mix that attempted to honour both the heritage of Christian worship and the changed make up of British society. The main feature was the requirement that all pupils take part in a daily act of worship which should be "wholly or mainly of a broadly Christian character". An act of worship was deemed to be broadly Christian if it "reflects the broad traditions of Christian belief" without being distinctive of any particular Christian denomination.

The situation was further complicated by the production of official guidance which was published in its final form in 1994 and is still in force.[32] This sought to clarify the nature of worship, describing it as "reverence or veneration paid to a divine being or power" alongside a definition that sought to embrace a broad understanding of what that worship entailed.[34] There was also a careful explanation that taking part meant more than passive attendance but didn't necessarily entail identification with the divine power or being. The document attempted to clarify what made an act of worship Christian, noting that according a special status to Jesus was integral. Finally, it stated that all children should be able to join in, presumably with the intention that their religious integrity should not be compromised even if they did not have a Christian background. Although with a much less complex statutory background, a similar situation existed in Scotland where Religious Observance was a required activity with the suggestion that this would reflect the Christian heritage of the country by being "of a broadly Christian character".

This complex, indeed bewildering, cacophony of legislation and guidance (only some of the technicalities it introduced have been mentioned here) caused much debate and considerable resentment amongst many educationalists.[37] It was felt that the tried and trusted assemblies that

> *Worship is "reverence or veneration paid to a divine being or power".*

characterized many schools had been hijacked by a Christian theological agenda carrying the force of law. It also resulted in some ludicrous legal manoeuvring, as when a judge ruled that the god worshiped in schools should be "God with a broadly Christian character."[38] Busy headteachers found it impossible either to understand or to implement. The key objection was that compulsory Christian worship was no longer an appropriate activity in the schools of a society where pupils came from backgrounds of many faiths and none. Many felt that something more inclusive was required.

In England and Wales there has only been one concerted attempt since 1988 to amend this tangle of regulations.[39] This took place in 1997 in a programme of three consultative conferences designed to ascertain whether there was a consensus for change among key players that could confidently be represented to government. The aspiration was to identify a formula that retained the positive benefits of the widely understood school assembly and which ensured that all pupils and staff "are able to share in good conscience" and was "as inclusive as possible".[40] In particular a way forward was considered that, it was suggested, might replace the 1988 requirements. It was:

a statutory requirement for regular assemblies of a spiritual and moral character, with the present requirement for collective worship being withdrawn. The main focus of these gatherings would be the promotion of reflection on values, beliefs and the spiritual dimension of life.[41]

Interestingly, in Scotland a similar formula was adopted when new guidance was issued in 2005. Religious Observance was redefined as "community acts which aim to promote the spiritual development of all members of the school community and express and celebrate the shared values of the school community".[42]

However, two things stand out when the Scottish documentation is compared to that considered by the 1997 consultation for England and Wales. Firstly, both had concerns about the appropriateness of worship in schools. However, in the Scottish context this was not that worship itself might be considered to be a toxic or anti-educational activity, but that the pupils' own faith integrity should be respected. The report that preceded the 2005 Scottish guidance therefore stated that acts of worship were entirely appropriate in a faith school where the religious character of the school was known to everyone who became part of that community, but not in schools that did not have a designated religious affiliation. The English and Welsh proposed revisions, however, seemed to assume that religious worship was, by definition, *an inappropriate activity in any educational context, even faith schools.*

Secondly, both grappled with the appropriateness of explicitly mentioning the Christian heritage that shaped the legislation being reviewed. The 2005 Scottish guidance encouraged schools "to use the rich resources of this tradition when planning religious observance", taking account of the need to respect the integrity of pupils and staff.[43] The 1997 English and Welsh documentation pointedly made no specific reference at all to Christianity in its recommendations, nor indeed to any faith.

> *The Scots treated the religious traditions as resources to be drawn on when appropriate in creating meaningful, inclusive assemblies.*

This is very significant. One of the recurring concerns expressed about the English and Welsh process was that the new, "inclusive" way forward would be a Trojan horse, effectively promoting the secularization of school assembly. The failure to discuss the importance of worship in church and other faith schools and the absence of discussion of how the new spiritual acts would embrace the distinctive religious traditions both seem to reflect the idea that, for assemblies to be inclusive in a plural society, religion has to be banished to the private realm. Instead, the focus is on the shared, apparently neutral, human characteristic of spiritual development. The underlying message is that religion, particularly Christianity in this case, is an irrelevance and a problem and that its exclusion will be to the educational benefit of all. The idea that religion is clutter in an inclusive approach to assemblies seems to be lurking in the background.

The English and Welsh 1997 consultation process foundered. Despite almost universal agreement in 1997 that the law and the guidance were not fit for purpose, the proposed way forward did not attract the required consensus to give the necessary confidence to propose it to government. Nothing has changed since 1997. In contrast, the 2005 Scottish changes appear to be succeeding. Maybe the difference is that the Scots treated the religious traditions as resources to be drawn on when appropriate in creating meaningful, inclusive assemblies, whereas the English and Welsh fell prey to the secularizing fear of religions that treated them as a problem to be marginalized. Is it too much to suggest that the Scots have succeeded in this most difficult area because they embraced a notion of "doing God" in education whereas the English and Welsh opted for excluding God?

conclusion

This chapter has explored what "doing God" in education might actually look like. MFL teaching provided an extended case study which demonstrated that religious beliefs are not "clutter", but actually make a significant difference to what happens in a classroom. It was also shown that so-called neutral teaching in MFL draws on specific and particular beliefs about the meaning and significance of learning in MFL. In particular, it prescribes a view of the relationship between language learner and native speaker, which itself implicitly assumes a certain model of what it means to be human. The beliefs which shape this are certainly secular in the sense of being non-religious, but they are not therefore neutral because they derive from a particular worldview. The chapter concluded by considering two hot topics in education policy – creationism and school worship. This discussion showed the continuing influence of the view that religious belief is clutter. In the final chapter, the positive benefits of resisting this influence will be explored.

chapter 3 references

1. David I Smith and Barbara Carvill, *The Gift of the Stranger: Faith, Hospitality and Language Learning* (Eerdmans, 2000) p. 154.

2. The word 'spiritual' is used here in the sense in which it is widely understood in educational parlance, describing a universal human characteristic. It is not to be understood as the same as religious.

3. Smith and Carvill, op cit, pp. 55-57.

4. Ibid, pp. 133-134.

5. Ibid, pp. 107-124.

6. Ibid, pp. 128-129. This is not to argue that teaching students the necessary skills for surviving as a tourist is wrong. Only to suggest that, if presented as the sole model of the relationship between language learner and native speaker, it is inadequate.

7. See Richard Layard and Judy Dunn, *A Good Childhood* (Penguin Books, 2009) and Richard Layard, *Happiness: lessons from a new science* (Penguin Books, 2005) for discussion of this contemporary culture.

8. Smith and Carvill, op cit, p. 121.

9. Ibid, p. 57.

10. Ibid, pp. 57-58.

11. Ibid, p. 88.

12. Ibid, p. 86.

13. Ibid.

14. Ibid, p. 107.

15. Ibid.

16. See David I Smith, *Learning from the Stranger: Christian faith and Cultural Diversity* (Eerdmans, 2009) for a fuller discussion.

17. Some argue that the phrase "authentically Christian" better captures the idea of faithfulness to Christian beliefs. This report uses the phrase "distinctively Christian" because of its current widespread use in educational circles, particularly in Church of England schools.

18. I am grateful to the staff of Southwell Minster School for introducing me to this idea.

19. A website with a range of similar examples is currently being developed by *The Transforming Lives Project*. This will be available towards the end of 2011. See www.transforminglives.org.uk for further details.

20. David I Smith, "On Viewing Learners as Spiritual Beings" paper presented at the CELT conference, Seattle Pacific University (19 March 2007) published in CELEA news, 1.1 (February, 2009). Available at http://www.calvin.edu/kuyers/files/arts/LearnersAsSpiritualCELEA.pdf.

21. See David Baker et al, *Charis Deutsch: Einheiten 1-5* (Association of Christian Teachers, 1996) for the teaching units.

22. Smith, *Learning from the Stranger,* op cit, p. 5.

23. Ibid, p. 6.

24. See Geoff Teece, "Is it learning about and from religions, religion or religious education? And is it any wonder that some teachers don't get it?" in *British Journal of Religious Education,* 32.2 (March 2010), for a discussion of this distinction within Religious Education.

25. David I Smith, "Students' Reading Practices and Spiritual Formation", paper presented at the Annual Stapleford Centre Theory of Education Conference (January, 2008) at the Hayes Conference Centre, Swanwick.

26. Ibid, p. 7.

27. Creationism here is taken to mean the belief that the natural world was created in accordance with a literal understanding of the account in the Book of Genesis in the Bible.

28. See for example "Creationism could be taught in schools under Tories, says Ed Balls", *Times Online* (21 November 2009) www.timesonline.co.uk/tol/news/politics/article6926283.ece.

29. *Guidance on the place of Creationism and Intelligent Design in Science Lessons.* Available at http://www.teachernet.gov.uk/_doc/11890/SJA%20Creationism%20Guidance%20180907%20final.doc.

30. For example on the Andrew Marr Show on 14 February 2010. See http://news.bbc.co.uk/1/hi/uk_politics/8514945.stm for the transcript of the interview.

31. See the press release at http://www.eauk.org/media/creationism-in-schools.cfm.

32. Circular 1/94 *Religious Education and Collective Worship,* (Department for Education, 31 January 1994). A very similar circular was produced for Welsh schools numbered 10/94.

33. Circular 1/94, op cit, para. 57.

34. Ibid, para. 50.

35. Ibid, para. 59.

36. Ibid, para. 63.

37. For a full discussion of the issues see The RE Council of England and Wales, *Collective Worship in Schools* (Culham Educational Foundation, 1996).

38. A High Court ruling by Justice McCullough on 26 February 1993.

39. See *Collective Worship Reviewed* (Culham College Institute, 1998) available at http://www.culham.ac.uk/Res_conf/cw_reviewed/index.html for the full account of the process.

40. Ibid, p. 18.

41. Ibid, p. 19.

42. See http://www.scotland.gov.uk/Publications/2004/05/19351/37058.

43. Ibid, para. 8.

doing God in education:
a way forward

This report has claimed that influential attempts to build an inclusive and fair education system by adopting a neutral approach which rejects "doing God" on the grounds that religious beliefs are "clutter" are misconceived. The challenges of undertaking education in a religiously plural democracy cannot be resolved so easily. The attempt to do so results in exclusion and unfairness because so-called neutrality in fact preferences a secular humanist understanding of what it means to be human over and against religious views. The report has proposed an alternative approach, which takes seriously the role that both religious and non-religious beliefs play in the development of human knowledge, as the way forward. This highlights the significance of the different interpretations of shared knowledge and values that people make, which are themselves shaped by the beliefs that they hold. To "do God" in education is to take this process of belief-inspired interpretation seriously. It is to allow religious believers to draw on their beliefs as equal partners with those who hold secular beliefs. What this might look like from one Christian perspective was explored through the case study of teaching modern foreign languages.

What actually holds society together?

Those who campaign for a neutral, secular approach to education do so because they are concerned for the future of mixed societies where people of many religious and non-religious convictions are citizens together. The important question they ask is what actually holds society together? They are rightly concerned as to how modern societies can be inclusive and cohesive. The advocates of a neutral approach look to concepts such as common humanity, rational knowledge and shared values to provide the glue for society. They interpret these as implying that religious beliefs should be treated as private "clutter" and therefore campaign for neutral, secular community schools for all children and against distinctive faith schools which, they argue, discriminate on religious grounds. The crucial challenge for their critics who argue for "doing God" is where this societal glue is to come from, given that allowing religion on to the public stage might well result in a discordant cacophony of voices singing conflicting songs about the nature of what it means to be human. The question is therefore how can education both be inclusive and embrace "doing God", given that the latter will inevitably highlight differences and the clash of beliefs?

A place for pragmatism?

A suggestion from the Humanist Philosophers' Group, which they call the pragmatic argument, is helpful here.[1] This draws on the idea of social contracts and emphasizes the disastrous consequences of people not agreeing. Their argument appeals to common interests and amounts to the suggestion that there are certain things that most people aspire to, such as peaceful coexistence and security, that can form the basis of the required societal glue. As the philosophers put it, "the lesson to be learned is that if people with different sets of religious and non-religious beliefs cannot learn to live together, the results are appalling for all parties".[2] Their suggestion is that focusing on common interests when shaping education policy is healthier and more beneficial all round than taking a final stand on our distinctive beliefs. Their case rests on the assumption that what is really important is "the will and ability to live well with those whose social space we share".[3] The pragmatic argument stakes its success on the hope that people will be persuaded to seek the well-being and flourishing of everyone within that social space.

For this to work, it is necessary that people do *in fact* agree that certain social goals are desirable. That this is the case can be illustrated, for example, by the evidence of an increasing shared concern about the experience of childhood in Britain. In 2007, this concern came to public attention with the publication of a UNICEF report which placed Britain last out of 21 of the world's richest countries in terms of children's well-being.[4] It was reinforced by *The Good Childhood Report* from the Children's Society, which identified excessive individualism as the underlying theme behind the many problems discussed.[5] This individualism fostered consumerism, aggression and unhealthy lifestyles.[6] The authors concluded that there is a need to change the overall ethos of society "making it less success-oriented and more generous with respect", describing this as promoting "the law of love".[7] Central to recovering this is, they suggest, a greater emphasis on the importance of values which offer "a vision of a good person and a good society".[8] They hope teachers might become "missionaries for harmonious living"[9] and help pupils to discover "the feeling of belonging to something bigger than yourself – something that gives meaning to one's small existence".[10]

Surveys suggest that it would probably not be that difficult to gain consensus on the importance of combating excessive individualism in the cause of promoting children's well-being.[11] Few teachers would argue with the importance of this. Indeed, schools make well-being a major focus of their work.[12] Most parents want their children to flourish and will largely agree on the values that will promote this. It seems that the appeal to pragmatism has teeth.[13]

On these grounds, the Humanist Philosophers' Group exhorts people to work together to improve children's well-being by accepting that state education should be neutral. Their argument appears to be: is it not better to be pragmatic and to privatize religion in order to achieve our shared aspirations rather than to attempt "doing God" in education and end up with conflict? Their appeal is: let's forget our differences of belief, they are just clutter that create problems; let's just focus on promoting well-being; we all know what that is.

The problem with this approach is that exactly what constitutes well-being as a human being is not the subject of agreement. Dig a bit deeper and one would find considerable difference in how well-being is interpreted lurking beneath the consensus that it is "a good thing". Humanists might interpret it in terms of free-thinking autonomy unencumbered by the toxic clutter of religious superstition. Muslims might understand it as achieved through submission to the will of Allah. Deep ecologists might advocate harmony with the natural world. Christians might interpret it as experienced through relationship with Christ. In the end the problem with the Humanist Philosophers' approach to pragmatism is that it rests on a secular understanding of well-being, which will be unacceptable to many with different convictions.

The fundamental difficulty with humanist pragmatism is that it starts from the premise that religious belief is the *problem* and that a secular, non-religious approach is the *solution*. But this is hardly going to feel fair and inclusive to religious people. Christians could equally argue that if we were all one in Christ the problems would be solved! Humanists' beliefs will obviously entail them viewing religion as a problem; that is inherent in the humanist view of things and has to be accepted as their position. However, this negative perception of religion seems increasingly to characterize the wider public view. The Archbishop of Canterbury commented on its influence in an interview in *The Daily Telegraph*. He said, "the trouble with a lot of government initiatives about faith is that they assume it's a problem, it's an eccentricity, it's practiced by oddities, foreigners and minorities."[14] The research on students training to be RE teachers mentioned previously certainly shows that Christians have somehow imbibed the idea that their faith is a problem and that they have to suppress it if they are to be professional RE teachers whereas atheists and agnostics apparently see their personal beliefs in a positive light and regard them as a professional resource.[15] But if the pragmatic argument really is to work, it cannot rely on demonizing the religious contribution to society.

> **Christians have somehow imbibed the idea that their faith is a problem and that they have to suppress it.**

There is an alternative approach to the pragmatic argument which treats religious (and non-religious) beliefs not as a problem to be dealt with by marginalizing them but as a potential resource that contributes social capital through promoting the common good. Research evidence that belonging to a faith community makes it more likely that young people will volunteer to support good causes provides justification for taking this view.[16] If it is accepted that everyone thinks from within a worldview, the alternative to privatizing it as problematic "clutter" is to welcome and affirm it as integral to being human. The alternative pragmatic argument would then encourage people to explore how their faith can support the common good and to listen to each other's beliefs in the cause of discovering truth and building a more harmonious society. The difference from the humanist pragmatic argument is that worldviews are, wherever possible, treated as a precious resource.

In this approach, people will be encouraged to identify the points where most people really do agree because their aspirations for society overlap. Promoting children's well being by combating excessive individualism is an example. The "bottom line" becomes not the willingness to privatize faith but the willingness to cooperate with those you disagree with in order to achieve the good of a relatively harmonious society where children can flourish through their experience of education.

"Doing God" is therefore a strategy for promoting *inclusive* education that draws on people's beliefs in the cause of the common good, in contrast to the anti-inclusive strategy of excluding God, which implicitly indoctrinates pupils into the idea that religion is "the problem". On this view public theology, understood as religious communities developing positive theologies that enable them to contribute as full partners in public life, should be actively encouraged in the cause of the common good. An example from the Christian tradition of what such theology might look like is as follows.[17]

harnessing the power of public theology

The Croatian-born theologian Miroslav Volf has reflected at length on how his Christian faith offers healing in the context of the religiously-based, tribal hatreds of the former Yugoslavia. He says that it was in Croatia "that the problem of identity and otherness fought and bled and burned its way into my consciousness".[18] As a professional theologian he felt that Christian faith ought to be able to offer another way for people to relate together when they were shaped by conflicting, strongly held identities. The future of humanity hung, in his view, on finding an alternative to the balkanisation which wrought such catastrophe in his native land. His pragmatic concern for alleviating human suffering drove him to uncover theological insights into situations of conflict, where people naturally tend to pursue the interest of their own identity over and against the interests of people with another identity. His conclusion was that the solution lay not in focussing, as policy makers tend to, on particular social arrangements, as for example in structuring education so that all schools are mixed, but in "fostering the kind of social agents capable of envisioning and creating just, truthful and peaceful societies and on shaping a cultural climate in which such agents will thrive".[19] In other words people's characters are ultimately more important than the institutions created by public policy. If Volf is right, educational policy should focus more on nurturing people with particular dispositions and providing an environment in which they can flourish, and not so much on forcing people to comply with certain structural arrangements (for example by abolishing faith schools and making every school a "neutral" community school).

For Volf, the Christian contribution to achieving this is to focus on the Cross, where the concepts of solidarity and of divine self-donation for the enemy are central. He is very aware of the historical complicity of Christian theology with domination in its seduction by the concept of Christendom, but his argument is that this mistaken approach had not comprehended the real significance of the Cross.[20] Rather a central motif of the Cross is embrace, reflected in the outstretched arms of Christ and encapsulated in the words of Paul in Romans: "Welcome one another, therefore, just as Christ has welcomed you" (15.7). He therefore regards social policies that entail exclusion as fundamentally un-Christian. However, he is also critical of some modern approaches to inclusion which refuse to recognize particularity, describing them as exclusion through assimilation. Provocatively he describes the offer made in such approaches to inclusion as: "We will refrain from vomiting you out if you let us swallow you up."[21]

Volf argues that the concept of embrace as reflected in Christ's work on the Cross is not some utopian aspiration to bring people together in a final reconciliation in the here-and-now but is, rather, simply a willingness to embrace those who are currently enemies. One emphasis of education should then be on developing the personal resources or dispositions people require in order to live together in peace in the absence of an immediate final reconciliation. The motivation for this is the expectation of a final reconciliation which is integral to Christian teaching on the last things.[22] Inspired by a vision of the future that God will ultimately bring about, Christians behave now in a way that foreshadows that future. Volf puts it as follows: "I will advocate here the struggle for a non-final reconciliation based on a vision of reconciliation that cannot be undone".[23] For this reconciliation to happen, people will need to embrace four key ideas: repentance, forgiveness, making space for the other and healing of memory. In this way the double exclusion of excluding my enemy from the community of humanity and myself from the community of sinners is banished and embrace becomes possible.

> No-one can be in the presence of the God of the crucified Messiah for long without overcoming this double exclusion – without transposing the enemy from the sphere of monstrous inhumanity into the sphere of shared humanity and herself from the sphere of proud innocence into the sphere of common sinfulness.[24]

Volf here is pointing out that people need both to stop seeing their neighbours as enemies and to stop seeing themselves as blameless if peace is to be possible. This change of attitude, he maintains, is inspired by a vision of the future reconciliation that is promised by God.

For the reader with no personal connection with Christian theology, much of this may seem bizarre. This impression will have been compounded by the attempt to condense a profound book of over 300 pages into a few paragraphs! None of this matters, however, because the purpose is not to convince the reader of the validity of this particular theology, but only to illustrate how Christian theologizing can support the aspiration for community cohesion and inclusion, and provide justification and motivation for Christians to support a pragmatic approach.[25] This, hopefully, should be enough to illustrate the importance of public theology. The sensible way to handle religious commitment in public education is not to treat it as irrelevant clutter, nor to paint it as a threat, but rather to view it as a resource to be harnessed, which can contribute exciting and fruitful perspectives on the pragmatically-agreed goals of public education. In this manner, "doing God" in education is of public benefit in winning the hearts and minds of religious believers to the cause of education which promotes human well-being. Public theology then contributes to society by fostering the development of a type of person who is motivated to work towards the common good.

two remaining challenges

Establishing that public theology provides positive social capital doesn't, however, take away the challenge that the clash of beliefs generates in educational contexts. In particular there are still the two questions of, firstly, how teachers as influential people in a position of power in relation to their pupils should handle their own commitment to strongly-held beliefs if they are not to be treated as a private matter, and secondly, of how faith schools can avoid the charge of discrimination.

1. professional conduct

Maybe it is fine for teachers to utilize their faith in developing educational approaches but many people would think it wrong for them to promote their own beliefs and thereby influence their pupils. Proselytizing is not appropriate in an inclusive and fair classroom. How then are those working in education to handle this challenge without compromising or abandoning their own beliefs?

Not surprisingly, one highly influential model is that teachers should be neutral, never revealing their own beliefs. As we have seen, research has shown that Christian student teachers feel particularly pressured to adopt this model, in contrast to their atheist colleagues who do not seem to have such inhibitions in expressing their views, regarding them as objective. This highlights the problem. Neutrality amounts to practical atheism.

The contrasting pragmatic approach advocated in this report recognizes the professional potential of the teacher's faith as an educational resource but also emphasizes the need for expression of that faith to be carefully managed in light of the sensitive and complex context of the modern school. An example of this approach is in the Code of Practice published by the RE Council of England and Wales in 2009, which outlined eight principles for handling religious and non-religious beliefs in schools.[27] The principles included "practice reciprocity", which encouraged teachers to behave in relation to other people's beliefs as they would hope others would behave towards their own beliefs, and "be open", which encouraged teachers to share their own beliefs in a manner that respected the needs of the pupils. Another example of a similar "code of practice" approach is the ethical guidelines for evangelism drawn up by the Christian-Muslim forum.[28] In these codes the emphasis is on being fair to other people and seeking to behave in ways that are inclusive and cooperative rather than being neutral.

Such codes of practice are products of a pragmatic approach which recognizes that education policy and practice in a religiously plural democracy have to be developed on the basis of a coalition between people of competing worldviews if they are ever to be fair. There is recognition of a shared goal, namely the educational value of teachers in a religiously-mixed context talking about their faith as a contribution to respecting diversity and valuing equality. However, there is also acknowledgement that this is controversial and potentially divisive and therefore needs managing in a professional manner. A code lays out both an agreed model of professionalism in a religiously plural public context and some practical guidance on how to achieve this.[29] Negotiating a professional code is an important element in developing an inclusive and fair pragmatic approach which recognizes both the positive contribution that people's religious and non-religious commitments can make in public education, and the conflict and hurt that can result if that contribution is not handled sensitively.

> *There needs to be a clear understanding of and commitment to the shared goal.*

To negotiate a code that will work there also needs to be a clear understanding of and commitment to the shared goal that is being pursued and a degree of trust in one's colleagues despite the, sometimes fundamental, differences of belief. That is personally very demanding. People are likely to feel hurt and offended as they experience each other's beliefs in their full candour. The alternative is to privatize beliefs and bury differences in a supposedly professional approach that treats faith as irrelevant to public life. There is little doubt that this appears to be the easier option. However, this report rejects this strategy on the grounds that it is not fruitful in building a successful plural society where difference is well-handled and the true role of belief in human knowledge is taken seriously. By treating religion as irrelevant clutter, the neutral approach drives people back into their private tribes and increases the likelihood of them leading parallel lives isolated from each other. A pragmatic approach based on "doing God", however, draws people into active participation in a religiously plural community where their beliefs are taken seriously.

There is no doubt that the approach commended in this essay is emotionally and spiritually demanding to implement. A person's worldview matters a lot to their personal identity and any challenge to that will often be experienced as a personal threat. To call people into "doing God" in education in a manner that honours fairness is to call them both to take those beliefs seriously in their professional life and to experience a degree of threat as they encounter others who hold beliefs that may well clash sharply with their own. This report rejects an approach which requires people to give first loyalty to professional norms in the name of alleged neutrality rather than to their personal beliefs,[30] but it does accept that these beliefs need managing professionally. What dispositions, then, are required of a social agent, to use Miroslav Volf's terminology, who can operate effectively as a professional in this educational environment?

There will of course be many; integrity, openness, authenticity, empathy, honesty and trustworthiness jump to mind. However, the concept of "courageous restraint" is one that invites particular attention as a replacement for the concept of dispassionate neutrality and its implied privatization of personal beliefs. Courageous restraint means that people are willing to stand back from what is naturally their first priority in order to respect the integrity of other people. It means being willing to let fairness temper one's advocacy of truth as you understand it. It means holding to the golden rule that one should treat other people as you hope they would treat you in similar circumstances. It means being willing to accept that the truth you personally hold dear is contestable in wider society. For the teacher in the classroom it means welcoming the expression of points of view by pupils and in the syllabus that you personally think are flawed, sometimes fundamentally so. For curriculum developers it will mean not looking simply to champion your own particular view, but being willing to introduce diversity of views into a syllabus. For policy makers it will mean allowing developments that may personally be seen as retrograde. The adjective *courageous* to describe this restraint is appropriate because the investment of personal identity that people make in their beliefs is such that it does take courage to restrain oneself from seeking their advantage. The difference between courageous restraint and neutrality is that the former does not treat personal beliefs as private and irrelevant. Rather it recognizes their significant place in being human. It has to be accepted, though, that there may come a point when such restraint can no longer be justified, at which point someone ceases to be able to participate willingly in the system and has to campaign against it. Then the coalition breaks down. But we are far from that point in twenty-first century Britain.[31]

2. faith schools

Faith schools are very controversial but they are also popular with government and parents. They are an excellent example of an educational policy which tests the exercise of courageous restraint.

Humanist opposition to faith schools is purportedly on the grounds that they are inherently discriminatory and the BHA therefore campaigns against them in principle. The Accord Coalition represents a less militant view which is not against faith schools *per se* but campaigns against alleged discriminatory practices, particularly in the admission of pupils and in the appointment of staff. However, there is also an underlying concern that faith schools are bad for community cohesion, encouraging the development of parallel communities and tribalistic attitudes because children and parents from different faith communities do not mix as they would in secular community schools. Here the spectre of Northern Ireland always looms large. Finally, there is also a concern that unhealthy attitudes based on narrow religious commitments will be propagated, for example in confessional approaches to religious education and sex and relationships education. Writing about the Conservative/Liberal Democrat Coalition's Academies Bill, Andrew Copson, the Chief Executive of the BHA, expressed his concern thus:

> Nothing in the new, deregulated system proposed by the bill would prohibit abstinence-based relationships education, or the teaching of creationism as a valid alternative to evolution, or the literal truth of a personal god.[32]

Leaving aside the highly controversial notions that schools should not encourage sexual abstinence amongst minors or teach about the literal truth of a personal god, the quote illustrates the concerns that faith schools engender.

The significant point that Copson makes elsewhere in this piece, however, is the charge that they discriminate against families and teachers by having religious criteria in their admissions and recruitment policies. This, he argues, is neither fair nor inclusive, particularly as the schools are funded by the tax payer. A similar concern was reflected in the Liberal Democrat manifesto for the May 2010 General Election which promised that, for new faith schools, the party would "develop an inclusive admissions policy and end unfair discrimination on grounds of faith when recruiting staff".[33]

Supporters of faith schools do have to answer this charge of discrimination if they are to also be advocates of a fair and inclusive education system. The assumption of the critics seems to be that *any form of selection using religious criteria is by definition discrimination (in a pejorative sense) and therefore unfair.* But why should this be? Selection for jobs and school places happens all the time, but is not considered discrimination as long as the criteria are relevant to the decisions being made. The opposition to selection in faith schools is based on the assumption that religion is an irrelevant criterion. But it has been argued throughout this report that this assumption that religion is clutter is wrong in its portrayal of the nature of human knowledge, ideological in its dependence on humanist beliefs and probably anti-religious in its negative view of faith. To utilise it as the defining feature for the charge of discrimination is, therefore, itself unfair and exclusive.

This report is not intended as an apologia for faith schools. The arguments advanced apply as much to the treatment of religion in community schools. However, if belief is as important in human knowledge as has been argued, it follows that faith schools make a lot of sense. In 2008, the Runnymede Trust, which describes itself as the leading race equality think tank, published the report *Right to Divide?* as its contribution to this debate.[34] This was unexpectedly positive towards the idea of faith schools, arguing that all parents should be given access to "what faith schools claim is a distinctive ethos".[35] Furthermore it recognized the important role of faith as "a marker of identity". The report's concern was to make the ethos of faith schools, which are very popular with parents, available for all in the community and not just to people from particular faith communities. The significant point is the report's assumption that a distinctive ethos is a benefit alongside the concern about selecting pupils and staff on the basis of that ethos.

There is a puzzle here. It is unclear how the distinctive ethos of a faith school is created if none of the students or staff is recruited on the basis that they hold that faith. This seems to suggest that religious belief is irrelevant "clutter" when it comes to creating a school's distinctive religious ethos. There is the ring of absurdity to a position which maintains that faith is integral to the school's ethos and then insisting that the community cannot recruit the people who understand and can create that ethos. Lack of attention to this aspect of faith-based institutions is what leads to them losing their distinctive ethos. The research evidence is that little attention has been given to this in schools with a Christian ethos in Britain.[37] The danger is that the faith label to a school actually means very little in identifiable distinctiveness, but becomes an excuse for the selection of more motivated and upwardly-mobile families who are prepared to attend church to gain access to the school, creating a successful school (in results terms) but not a distinctive school (in faith terms). That *would* be unfair discrimination and would certainly not reflect a Christian aspiration for running schools.

In *Right to Divide?* Rob Berkeley challenges faith schools to become schools for all and to "develop teaching practices and ideologies that value everyone equally".[38] He wants them to use the resource offered by their distinctiveness to become "schools for all in the community rather than a means of ensuring exclusivity".[39] This is where Miroslav Volf and other theologians have much to offer. In practical terms this means that faith schools have to work hard at developing a distinctive faith ethos that makes all pupils and staff feel welcome and full members of the school community. It also means welcoming other points of view as opportunities for learning and enrichment, and developing strategies to ensure these are represented and heard.[40] This clearly has implications for admissions and recruitment policies. Selection criteria that honour the need to create the school ethos and selection criteria that ensure that diversity is represented will probably *both* be necessary. The skill is in achieving an appropriate balance between selecting those who can create and develop the distinctive ethos and those who will contribute another perspective. *What this does do is make faith an essential factor to consider not irrelevant clutter.* Creating a faith-inspired hospitable culture will, however, make huge demands on the school's staff who, no doubt, will each

> *It is unclear how the distinctive ethos of a faith school is created if none of the students or staff is recruited on the basis that they hold that faith.*

and all have to exercise "courageous restraint" in managing their understandable enthusiasm for their own faith.[41]

A final metaphor offers a vision for a distinctive faith culture that is inclusive. St Ethelburga's Church in the City of London was bombed by Irish Republican terrorists in 1993. When it was rebuilt it became a centre of reconciliation. In its grounds is a nomadic tent called the "tent of meeting". This has become a place where people of different faiths meet together to consider issues of common concern, to share insights from their own scriptures, to explore the differences between them and to look for ways of cooperating together in solving problems. In this context faith is certainly not irrelevant clutter. Rather it is an invaluable resource. This is not a neutral space, being in the grounds of a Christian church. But it is an inclusive, mutual space where Christian hospitality aspires to be as fair as possible. Maybe the "tent of meeting" is an appropriate metaphor for the distinctive ethos of a faith school?[42]

conclusion

Religious faith is too important an influence in human life to be ignored in education. To treat it as a problem that is only studied in RE is to assume that secularism is the only worldview that has the potential to be social glue in a diverse society. That is not an inclusive or fair approach, nor is it wise, if the religiously diverse society that Britain is now is to flourish.

> *"Doing God" in education offers the potential of a positive contribution to promoting human flourishing.*

"Doing God" in education need not be the sectarian exercise its critics fear. Rather it offers the potential of a positive contribution to promoting human flourishing. Of course, pragmatic commitment to the importance of living and learning successfully alongside fellow citizens who may well be opponents in faith will be essential. That will require courageous restraint on everyone's part.

chapter 4 references

1. Humanist Philosophers' Group, *The Case for Secularism* (British Humanist Association, 2007) pp. 14-16.

2. Ibid, p. 14.

3. Stephen Backhouse, *Red, White, Blue….and Brown, citizens, patriots and the Prime Minister* (Theos, 2007) p. 50.

4. UNICEF, *Child Poverty in Perspective: An Overview of Child well-Being in Rich Countries* (2007).

5. Richard Layard and Judy Dunn, *A Good Childhood: Searching for values in a Competitive Age* (Penguin, 2009) p. 4.

6. Ibid, p. 54.

7. Ibid, p. 135.

8. Ibid, p. 78.

9. Ibid, p. 82.

10. Ibid, p. 84.

11. See http://www.socialevils.org.uk/ for the major research project carried out by the Joseph Rowntree Foundation on what people in Britain perceived as the social evils of today.

12. The *Every Child Matters* programme makes this a statutory duty for English schools.

13. See for example the successful work of the National Forum for Values in 1996 discussed in chapter 2.

14. Martin Beckford and George Pitcher "Archbishop of Canterbury: 'Labour treats us like oddballs'", *The Daily Telegraph* (12 December 2009), http://www.telegraph.co.uk/news/newstopics/religion/6792088/Archbishop-of-Canterbury-Labour-treats-us-like-oddballs.html.

15. Lynn Revell & Rosemary Walters, *Christian Student RE Teachers, objectivity and professionalism* (Canterbury Christ Church University, 2010).

16. See Susannah Clark and Justin Thacker, *Young People Matter* (Evangelical Alliance, 2009) and James Arthur, Robert Harding and Ray Godfrey, *Citizens of Character* (University of Birmingham, 2009).

17. See Sean Oliver-Dee, *Religion and identity: Divided loyalties?* (Theos, 2009) for a discussion relating to Islam.

18. Miroslav Volf, *Exclusion and Embrace* (Abingdon Press, 1996) p. 16.

19. Ibid, p. 21.

20. See Nick Spencer, *Neither Private nor Privileged: The Role of Christianity in Britain Today* (Theos, 2008), especially chapter 1, for a critique of the theocratic model.

21. Volf, op cit, p. 75.

22. See NT Wright, *Surprised By Hope* (SPCK, 2007) and *Virtue Reborn* (SPCK, 2010) for examples of how eschatological reflection can contribute to building a person with particular dispositions in the here-and-now.

23. Ibid, p. 110.

24. Ibid, p. 124.

25. For other examples of harnessing Christian theology in education see Trevor Cooling, "Go and Make Disciples: education as Christian Mission" in *Journal of Christian Education* 51.2 (2008) pp. 5-22 and David I Smith, *Learning from the Stranger* (Eerdmans, 2009). For examples of other approaches to public theology in general which do this see Stephen Backhouse, *Red, White, Blue…and Brown: citizens, patriots and the Prime Minister* (Theos, 2007) which utilizes the theme of neighbourliness and Luke Bretherton, *Hospitality as Holiness: Christian witness amid moral diversity* (Ashgate Publishing Limited, 2006), which utilizes the concept of hospitality.

26. Revell & Walters, op. cit.

27. The General Teaching Council for England published a code of conduct in 2009 that makes promoting equality and respecting diversity a professional duty. See http://www.gtce.org.uk/teachers/thecode/. *Everyone Matters in the Classroom* is a development of this which explicitly addresses how to handle religious and non-religious beliefs in the classroom. See http://www.religiouseducationcouncil.org/content/blogcategory/50/80/.

28. http://www.christianmuslimforum.org/downloads/Ethical_Guidelines_for_Witness.pdf.

29. See Chaplin, op cit (2008) chapter 5, where he develops the principles of candour in representation and restraint in decision making for managing of religious beliefs in the public realm. Here Chaplin is in effect suggesting principles for a professional code of conduct.

30. For further discussion of the inadequacy of the so-called sacred-secular divide approach see Trevor Cooling & Mark Greene, *Supporting Christians in Education* (London Institute for Contemporary Christianity, 2008) chapter 2.

31. Nick Spencer discusses this point in *Neither Private nor Privileged: the Role of Christianity in Britain Today* (Theos, 2008). For further discussion of the implications of the ideas of coalition and restraint see Trevor Cooling, *A Christian Vision for State Education* (SPCK, 1994), "The Challenge of Passionate Religious Commitment for School Education in a World of Religious Diversity" in *Journal of Education & Christian Belief*, 11.1 (2007) pp. 23-34 and "Education" in Rose Lynas (ed), *Votewise now!* (SPCK, 2009).

32. Andrew Copson, "An open door to religious academies", *The Guardian*, 11 June 2010. See http://www.guardian.co.uk/commentisfree/belief/2010/jun/11/religion-academies-bill-education.

33. See Liberal Democrats manifesto (2010) p. 37 at http://issuu.com/libdems/docs/manifesto.

34. Rob Berkeley, *Right to Divide,* Runnymede Trust, 2008. See http://www.runnymedetrust.org/uploads/publications/pdfs/RightToDivide-2008.pdf.

35. Ibid, p. 4.

36. See James Arthur, *Faith and Secularisation in Religious Colleges and Universities* (Routledge, 2006).

37. See Elizabeth Green and Trevor Cooling, *Mapping the Field: a review of the current research evidence on the impact of schools with a Christian ethos* (Theos, 2009).

38. Berkeley, op cit, p. 5.

39. Ibid.

40. See David I Smith, *Learning from the Stranger* (Eerdmans, 2009).

41. For a fascinating account of a Christian school that treated this as a professional development issue for its staff see John Collier and Martin Dowson, "Applying an Action Research Approach to Improving the Quality of Christian Education", *Journal of Christian Education*, 50.1 (2007) pp. 27-36.

42. http://stethelburgas.org/our-story/tent.

some implications

This report has focussed on the fundamental issues that underpin the debates about the place of religious and non-religious worldviews in education. This chapter outlines some implications as to the practices that will follow from the conclusions reached. It would, of course, require another separate report to pursue these in any depth in relation to faith schools, RE, the place of faith in the other subjects, school worship, and parental choice. However, to give a flavour of some of the consequences of adopting the suggested approach, a few suggestions, neither comprehensive nor prioritized, follow below. The reader is invited to add some of their own.

In relation to teachers, it should be part of the professional culture that all teachers, not just those of religious faith, are required to consider the impact of their own worldview on their work. Teachers' handling of their own worldview beliefs should be guided through a code of conduct which exemplifies professional behaviour and, in particular, encourages a balance between passionate commitment and courageous restraint. Teacher training programmes should introduce trainee teachers to the knowledge, understanding and skills required to deal with belief and diversity.

> *It should be part of the professional culture that all teachers are required to consider the impact of their own worldview on their work.*

In relation to learning, the fundamental role of worldviews in human learning should be acknowledged throughout education. In schools that don't have a religious character, this will mean that consideration of the impact of worldviews will happen across the curriculum, and not be restricted to RE. In faith schools, the curriculum should be developed in line with the distinctive ethos, taking account of the need to introduce pupils to the diversity of beliefs that exist in society.

In relation to faith schools, the BHA should suspend its campaign against such schools and instead agitate for high quality education within them, education that draws on the resources of faith in the service of the wider community. School admissions on the basis of religious affiliation should be maintained alongside admissions policies that enable the diversity of society also to be reflected. Staff selection for faith schools on the basis of religious philosophy is appropriate as long as commitment to the goals of public education is maintained and the diversity of society as a whole is reflected. Faith schools should promote a philosophy of active and cooperative citizenship among their pupils.

In relation to RE, humanism should be taught as a significant worldview in RE and humanists should be full members of Standing Advisory Councils for RE. RE teachers should support their colleagues in other subjects to ensure that God-talk (or worldview talk) is not restricted to RE.

In relation to school worship, it should be regarded as a positive opportunity to engage with the significance of the religious dimension of life in today's world and not treated as an anachronistic relic. Careful thought will need to be given to the appropriateness of the current regulations and practices. In particular the excellent practice that exists in some schools should be disseminated with a view to enabling all schools to provide meaningful assemblies that engage pupils with the significance of religious and non-religious beliefs and practices and encourage them to develop as spiritual beings.

The current debate is often presented in the media as a confrontation between the sectarian interests of faith communities and those who care about decent education for children.[1] This is both unfair and unhelpful. This report is a plea for a more co-operative approach where religious and non-religious people work together in education for the benefit of the pupils and of society as a whole. For this to happen, however, we are all going to have to swallow hard and rely less on our soap boxes and more on our negotiating skills.

chapter 5 references

1. For example the programme *Faith Schools Menace?* presented by Richard Dawkins on More4 on 17 August 2010.

C O M M O N S   D E E D

Attribution-NonCommercial-NoDerivs 2.5

You are free:

- to copy, distribute, display, and perform the work

Under the following conditions:

Attribution. You must attribute the work in the manner specified by the author or licensor.

Noncommercial. You may not use this work for commercial purposes.

No Derivative Works. You may not alter, transform, or build upon this work.

- For any reuse or distribution, you must make clear to others the license terms of this work.
- Any of these conditions can be waived if you get permission from the copyright holder.

Your fair use and other rights are in no way affected by the above.